Table of Contents

MW01028501

Neural Networks: A Visual Introduction for Beginners by Michael Taylor

Published by Blue Windmill Media

© 2017 Blue Windmill Media

Blue Windmill Media

For permissions contact:

matthew@bluewindmill.co

We love reviews! Let us know your thoughts on Amazon or via email: matthew@bluewindmill.co

Cover by Blue Windmill Media

What You'll Find Inside:

200 + Easy-To-Read Images

This book is a visual introduction with over 200 images that are formatted specifically for print. This means you don't need to squint or struggle to read formulas or understand details.

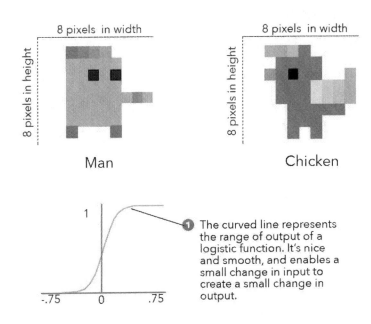

8 pixels in width
8 pixels in height
Man

8 pixels in width
8 pixels in height
Chicken

1

-.75   0   .75

The curved line represents the range of output of a logistic function. It's nice and smooth, and enables a small change in input to create a small change in output.

A Beginner-Friendly Approach

This book is designed for beginners, which is why we explain every detail line-by-line. This means that we do not gloss over lines of code or assume you understand all of the elements in a formula.

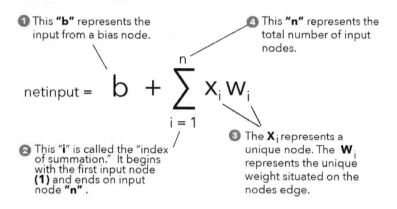

1 This **"b"** represents the input from a bias node.

4 This **"n"** represents the total number of input nodes.

$$\text{netinput} = b + \sum_{i=1}^{n} x_i w_i$$

2 This "**i**" is called the "index of summation." It begins with the first input node (**1**) and ends on input node "**n**" .

3 The x_i represents a unique node. The w_i represents the unique weight situated on the nodes edge.

$$\delta_b = \left(\sum_{c} \delta_z w_i \right) \text{out}_i (1 - \text{out}_i)$$

5 All of the letter "**i**"'s refer to a unique value. This value depends on the gradient we are calculating.

Don't Waste Your Time

A few points to help you make the most of this book:

1. *This book is designed as a visual introduction to neural networks. It is for BEGINNERS and those who have minimal knowledge of the topic.* If you already have a general understanding, you might not get much out of this book.

2. *You don't need to read front to back.* Skip around to what you find the most helpful or is perking your interest.

3. We *slowly* layer in new terminology and concepts each chapter. This means that if you jump to chapter 4 without having read chapter 3, you might come across terminology that you do not understand. Be aware of this, and remember: you can always jump back to clarify a topic or concept.

Part 1
Neural Networks

Ch. 1
What is a Neural Network? A Brief Overview

Neural networks have made a gigantic comeback in the last few decades and you likely make use of them everyday without realizing it, but *what exactly is* a neural network? What is it used for and how does it fit within the broader arena of machine learning?

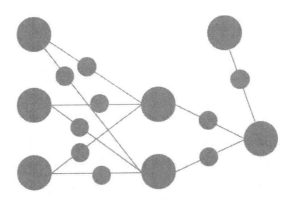

A Basic Neural Network

In this chapter we are going to gently explore these topics so that we can be prepared to dive deep further on. To start, we'll begin with a high-level overview of machine learning and then drill down into the specifics of a neural network.

Machine Learning

Machine learning is the science of getting computers to act without being explicitly programmed, and it is our biggest step towards making artificial intelligence a reality. If you like movies, think *Ex Machina* or *Transcendence* or *I, Robot* - but just the good parts! Machine learning is a field within computer science that has gained incredible traction within the last few decades and it likely touches your life everyday.

From Google search to Uber rides and YouTube ads, machine learning is not only a buzzword but also increasingly being tested and used in countless industries to improve speed, reduce errors and boost efficiency.

Machine learning is all about algorithms - or rules - that are used to work with data and make predictions. For example, email providers such as *Yahoo!* and *Gmail* use algorithms to filter your email and keep spam out of your inbox.

On a high-level, spam filtering algorithms achieve this by being trained on what *is spam* and *is not spam*. For this to happen, the algorithm is fed thousands of emails labelled as spam and not spam, and after analyzing each email, the algorithm eventually "learns" how to spot spam by identifying common characteristics that separate it from legitimate, real email. These characteristics could be certain phrases or words, such as "earn per week", "no strings attached" or even "vacation".

There are many types of machine learning algorithms that are currently used, and there are a variety of ways they can be categorized. One of the easiest to understand is grouping by similarity and learning style.

Similarity:

Similarity	Algorithm Ex #1	Algorithm Ex #2
Regression	Logisitc Regression	Linear Regression
Decision Tree	CART	ID3
Clustering	Naive Bayes	Gaussian Naive Bayes
Neural Networks	Back Propagation	Convolutional (CNN)

* This list is not comprehensive. There are many more algorithms and similarity categories.

Learning Style

On a high level, there are three popular ways that machine learning can be approached:

#1: Supervised Learning

With supervised learning, the learning algorithm is presented with a set of inputs along with their desired outputs (also called labels). The goal is to discover a rule that enables the computer to re-create the outputs, or in other words, *map* the input to output.

For example, think of categorizing images of cats and dogs. To teach an algorithm what a dog is and a cat is, an algorithm would be presented with thousands of images of each, and each image would be labelled as "dog" or "cat".

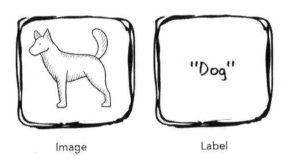

Image   Label

This label is the desired output for each image, and by analyzing each example the algorithm would eventually be able to classify new images of cats and dogs with very minimal error. *In reality this label is not a written word such as "Dog" or "Cat", but a numerical representation of each label. We'll dive more into this further on.

#2: Unsupervised Learning

With unsupervised learning, an algorithm is presented with a set of inputs but *no desired outputs*, which means the algorithm must find structure and patterns *on its own*. To link this to the supervised example above, if images of dogs and cats were fed into an unsupervised algorithm, each image would not have a label that identifies it as a "cat" or "dog".

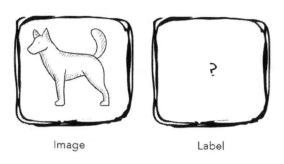

Image   Label

Instead, the algorithm would have to find patterns on its own as it assess the thousands of dog and cat images. Patterns could be the length of the animal, height, etc.

#3 Semi-Supervised Learning

Semi-supervised learning (SSL) is a mixture of the previous two learning styles, which means it is fed a combination of labelled and unlabelled inputs. Practically speaking, this means that SSL algorithms must find structure and patterns on their own but do have some help from labelled inputs.

A great example is web page classification into categories such as "shopping" or "news". It would be extremely expensive and time-consuming to hire a team to manually label thousands of websites, but an alternative does exist: labelling a small subset of websites. With SSL, this small subset would be fed into an algorithm as the "labelled" set alongside thousands of other websites that are not labelled. The algorithm could be trained on the unlabeled set first before being fine-tuned with the labelled set.

Neural Networks

A neural network, also known as an artificial neural network, is a type of machine learning algorithm that is inspired by the biological brain. It is one of many popular algorithms that is used within the world of machine learning, and its goal is to solve problems in a similar way to the human brain.

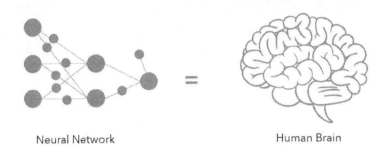

Neural Network   Human Brain

Neural networks are part of what's called Deep Learning, which is a branch of machine learning that has proved valuable for solving difficult problems, such as recognizing things in images and language processing.

Neural networks take a different approach to problem solving than that of conventional computer programs. To solve a problem, conventional software uses an algorithmic approach, i.e. the computer follows a set of instructions in order to solve a problem.

In contrast, neural networks approach problems in a very different way by trying to mimic how neurons in the human brain work. In fact, they learn by example rather than being programmed to perform a specific task.

Technically, they are composed of a large number of highly interconnected processing elements (nodes) that work in parallel to solve a specific problem, which is similar to how the human brain works.

Now, there is a lot that can be said about neural networks, but since this is an overview, here are the top 5 things you should know:

#1. Neural Networks Are Specific

Neural networks are always built to solve a specific type of problem, although this doesn't mean they can be used as "general purpose" tools. For example, you will not find a "general purpose" algorithm that you can sink data into for prediction or estimation...at least not yet!

Examples of specific uses include:
- Prediction
- Forecasting
- Classification
- Pattern recognition

Real world examples include: Stock market prediction, real estate appraisal, medical diagnosis, handwriting recognition, and recognizing images.

#2. Neural Networks Have 3 Basic Parts:
A neural network has three basic sections, or parts, and each part is composed of "nodes".

1. Input Layer
2. Hidden Layer(s)
3. Output Layer

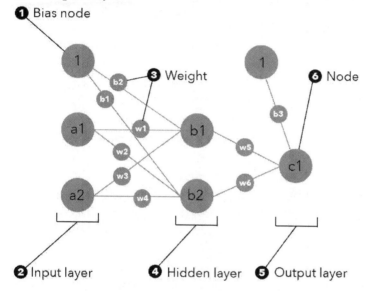

#3. Neural Networks Are Built 2 Ways
On a high level, neural networks can be built two ways:

1. **Feedforward:** With a feedforward neural network, signals travel only one way, from input to output. These types of networks are more straightforward and used extensively in pattern recognition. A convolutional neural network (CNN or ConvNet) is a specific type of feedforward network that is often used in image recognition.

2. **Feedback (or recurrent neural networks, RNNs):** With an RNN, signals can travel both directions and there can be loops. Feedback networks are more powerful and complex than CNNs, and they are always changing. Despite this, RNNs have been less influential than feedforward networks, in part because the learning algorithms for recurrent nets are (at least to date) less

powerful. However, RNNs are still extremely interesting and are much closer in spirit to how our brains work than feedforward networks.

#4. Neural Networks Are Either Fixed or Adaptive

Neural networks can be either fixed or adaptive.

1. **Fixed**: The weight values in a fixed network remain static. They do not change.
2. **Adaptive**: The weight values in an adaptive network are not static and can change.

#5. Neural Networks Use 3 Types of DataSets

Neural networks are often built and trained using three datasets:

- **Training dataset:** The training dataset is used to adjust the weights of the neural network.
- **Validation dataset:** The validation dataset is used to minimize a problem known as overfitting, which we will cover in more detail.
- **Testing dataset:** The testing dataset is used as a final test to gauge how accurately the network has been trained.

These three sets are usually taken from one very large dataset that represents the "gold standard" of data for a project, and are often split 60/20/20:

Training data: 60%
Validation data: 20%
Testing data: 20%.

EVERYBODY JUST WANTS *to be* LOVED

Show Astro Robot some love and
DROP US AN EMAIL
or
LEAVE A REVIEW
and let us know how we did!

Part 2
The Math of Neural Networks

The Math of Neural Networks: Introduction

There are many reasons why neural networks fascinate us and have captivated headlines in recent years. They make web searches better, organize photos, and are even used in speech translation. Heck, they can even generate encryption. At the same time, they are also mysterious and mind-bending: how exactly do they accomplish these things ? What goes on *inside* a neural network?

On a high level, a network learns just like we do, through trial and error. Once we dig a bit deeper though, we discover that a handful of mathematical functions play a major role in the trial and error process. It also becomes clear that a grasp of the underlying mathematics helps clarify *how a network learns.*

This is why the following chapters will be devoted to understanding the mathematics that drive a neural network. To do this, we will use a feedforward network as our model and follow input as it moves through the network.

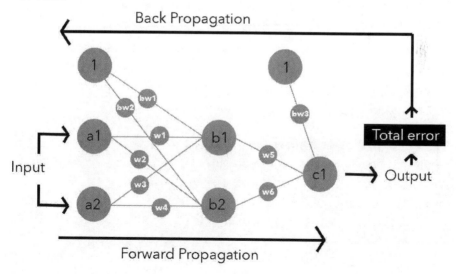

This "process" of moving through the network is complex though, so to make it easier and bite-size, we will divide it into 5 stages and take it slow.

Each of the stages includes at least one mathematical function, and we will devote an entire chapter to every stage. Our goal is that by the end, you will find neural networks less mind-bending and simply more fascinating. What's more, we hope that you'll be able to confidently explain these concepts to others and make use of them for yourself.

Here are the stages we will be exploring:

Stage 1: Forward Propagation
Required: Summation operator
Required: Activation function

Stage 2: Calculate the Total Error
Required: Cost function

Stage 3: Calculate the Gradients
Required: Partial derivative
Required: Chain Rule

Stage 4: Gradient Checking
Required: Gradient checking formula

Stage 5: Updating Weights
Required: Weight update formula

However, before diving into the stages, we are going to clarify the terminology and notation that we will be using. We will also take a moment to build on the topics and ideas introduced in the previous chapters. Accomplishing these things will build up a solid framework and provide us with the tools required to move forward.

A extra few words before moving on:
You might be scratching your head and wondering if all networks have the same mathematical functions. The answer is a loud *no*, and for a few good reasons, including the network architecture, its purpose, and even the personal preferences of its developer. However, there is a general framework for feedforward models that includes a handful of mathematical functions, which is what we will be investigating.

On another note, the following chapters require a college-level grasp of algebra, statistics and calculus. A major concept you'll come across is calculating partial derivatives, which itself makes use of the chain rule. Please be aware of this! If you are rusty in these areas you might find yourself repeatedly frustrated. The Khan Academy offers top-notch free courses in algebra, calculus and statistics. Visit the Khan Academy at https://www.khanacademy.org/.

Ch. 3

Terminology and Notation

If you are new to the field of neural networks or machine learning in general, one of the most confusing aspects can be the terminology and notation used. Textbooks, online lectures, and papers often vary in this regard.

To help minimize potential frustration we have put together a few charts to explain what you can expect in this book.

The first is a list of common terms used to describe the same function, object or action, along with a clarification of which term we will be using. The second list contains common notation, along with a clarification of the notation we will be using. Hopefully this helps!

Note: The majority of these terms will be explained throughout each stage. However, you can always take a peek at our extended definitions section for additional help.

Terms:

Term	We Will be Using
Activation Function / Transfer Function	Activation Function
Artificial Neural Network / Neural Network	Neural Network
Learning Algorithm / Learning Rule	Learning Algorithm
Node / Neuron	Node
Synapse / Edge / Connection	Edge
Target / Taret Output / Ideal Output / Desired Output / Target Pattern	Target Output

The notation chart is below. You might find it helpful to bookmark the page for reference.

Notation	Common Usage	We Will be Using
x	Denotes network input. Ex: x_1, x_2, x_3,....x_n	The letter **a**. Ex: a_1, a_2, a_3,....a_n
$\hat{y}$ or z	Denotes total network output.	z
n or m	Denotes number of training examples.	n
$\sigma(x)$ or $\phi(x)$	Denotes the logistic activation function, which computes the output of a node.	On a high level, we will use $\sigma(x)$. When computing partial derivatives, we will use the syntax **outb1**, where b1 is the node we are calculating the output for.
J(W) or $J(\theta)$	Denotes the cost function, which is the total error of the network.	On a high level we will use the phrase **total error**. We will also use a capital **E** when calculating partial derivatives.
$\sum$	Denotes the summation operator , which computes the net input of a node.	On a high level we will use $\sum$. When computing partial derivatives we will use the syntax **netb1**, were b1 is the node we are calculating the input for.
η	Denotes the learning rate.	η
$W_{ji}^{(1)}$	Denotes a weight in the first layer going from input **i** to hidden **j**.	We will refer to weights with numbers. Ex: $\tilde{W}_5$
t_i and z_i	Denotes the target and actual output of a single output node.	t_i and z_i
θ_w	Denotes a specific weight within a vector.	θ_w

Ch. 4

Pre-Stage: Creating the Network Structure

In the previous chapters, we touched on a variety of neural network architectures such as CNNs and RNNs. Although each is slightly different, all have a structure - or shell - that is made up of similar parts. These parts are called *hyperparameters*, and include elements such as the number of layers, nodes and the learning rate.

Hyperparameters are essentially fine tuning knobs that can be tweaked to help a network successfully train. In fact, they are determined before a network trains, and can only be adjusted manually by the individual or team who created the network. The network itself does not adjust them.

You can see some of these hyperparameters in the feedforward network below:

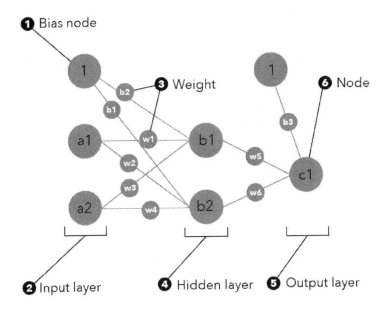

In this chapter we are going to take a brief pause to explore these hyperparameters because they are extremely important. Not only are they tuning knobs that help a network train, but all of a networks mathematical calculations depend on them being in place. We will begin by defining the two categories of hyperparameters, and then briefly explore each.

Types of Hyperparameters
Broadly speaking there are two categories of hyperparameters: required and optional.

Required Hyperparameters Include:

- Total number of input nodes
- Total number of hidden layers
- Total number of hidden nodes in each hidden layer
- Total number of output nodes
- Weight values
- Bias values
- Learning Rate

Optional Hyperparameters Include:*

- Learning rate schedule (a.k.a learning rate decay)
- Momentum
- Mini-batch size
- Weight decay
- Dropout

*This list is not exhaustive !

Now, let's take a brief look at each of the required hyperparameters. Please note that many new terms will be introduced below, and we will explain each as we move throughout the stages.

Input Node
An input node contains the *input* of the network and this input is *always* numerical. If the input is not numerical by default, it is always converted. For example:

- Images are often converted to grayscale, and each pixel is measured on a scale of 0 to 1 for intensity (where 0 (zero) is black, and 1 is white).
- Text is converted to numbers. For example, male/female might be converted to 1 and 0 (zero), respectively.
- Sound is converted to numbers that represent amplitude across time, with 0 (zero) when silent and 1 when loud.
-

An input node is located within the input layer, which is the first layer of a neural network. Each input node represents a single *dimension* and is often called a *feature,* and all features are stored within a *vector*.

For example, if you have an image of 16x16 pixels as input, you have a total of 256 input nodes. This is because each input node represents a single image pixel, and there are 256 pixels in total (16x16).

Now, in light of the descriptive language available, there are multiple ways an input vector can be described, including:
- 256 nodes
- 256 features
- 256 dimensions

The terminology can be quite heavy, so we will keep to using *node* in this book!

Hidden Layer

A hidden layer is a layer of nodes between the input and output layers. There can be either a single hidden layer or multiple hidden layers in a network, and the more that exist, the "deeper" the learning that a network can perform. In fact, multiple hidden layers are what the term *deep learning* refers to. Selecting the number of hidden layers is a complex topic and beyond the scope of our overview.

Hidden Node

A hidden node is a node within a hidden layer. A hidden layer can have *many hidden* nodes, and there are various theories for implementing the correct amount. General rules of thumb coupled with trial and error are what guide most data scientists and programmers. Studies have demonstrated that layers which contain the same amount of nodes generally performed the same *or better* than a decreasing *or* increasing pyramid shaped network. We won't go any deeper than that!

Output Node

An output node is a node within an output layer. There can be a single or multiple output nodes depending on the objective of the network. For example, if a network exists to classify handwritten digits from 0 to 9, there would be 10 output nodes (0 (zero) is one of them, hence there are 10 output nodes). Similar to the input of a network, the output is a *vector*.

Weight Value

A weight is a variable that sits on an *edge* between nodes. The output of every node in a layer is multiplied by a weight, then summed with other weighted nodes in that layer to become the *net input* of a node in the following layer. Weights are important because they are the primary *tuning knob* that is used to train a network.

Algorithms are typically used to assign random weights for a neural network. A popular range is between -1 and 1.

Bias Value

A bias node is an extra node added to each hidden and output layer, and it connects to every node within each respective layer. A bias is never connected to a previous layer, but is simply added to the input of a layer. In addition, it typically has a constant value of 1 or -1 and has a weight on its connecting edge.

Technically, the bias provides every node in a neural network with a trainable constant value (1 or -1). On a practical level, this enables the activation function to be shifted to the left or right. Alongside the adjusting of weights, this "shifting" can be very important and critical for successful learning. We will cover activation functions in more detail later on!

Below is an example of the Logistic (Sigmoid) activation function plotted on a graph. It is a fantastic visualization of how a bias can help "shift" the output of a node, and ultimately help a network successfully train.

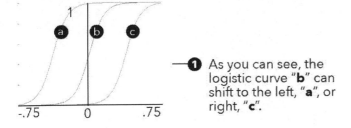

❶ As you can see, the logistic curve "**b**" can shift to the left, "**a**", or right, "**c**".

Learning Rate

The learning rate is a value that speeds up or slows down how quickly an algorithm learns. Technically, it determines the size of step an algorithm takes when moving towards a *global minimum,* i.e., the lowest error rate. *Although in practice, the global minimum is often not reached and the algorithm settles for a local minimum that is close to the global.

A learning rate can be static and remain consistent throughout the learning process, or it can be programmed to scale down as the network's error rate falls. A few more points to consider:

- There are multiple theories on how to select a proper learning rate, but in most cases selection will depend on trial and error.
- A learning rate that is too high can impact a networks ability to converge - or in other words, it will fail to reach a *global minimum.* It can also cause the network to overshoot and/or diverge. See below for an example of what divergence looks like. Note that with divergence, the lowest point (bottom of "U" shaped surface) is never reached. Instead, the network "bounces" around and never reaches the bottom.

❶ Diverging can occur when the learning rate is too large.

- A learning rate that is too low can cause a network to take a *long time* to converge.

Most study cases you will find online make use of learning rates close to 0 (zero), such as 0.1.

Momentum

Momentum is a value that is used to help push a network out of a *local minimum,* which is a false "lowest-error" that networks often become trapped in. Technically, momentum must be predetermined for the network, and is also one of the most popular techniques added to backpropagation. Momentum and backpropagation will be discussed in detail further on.

Now onto Stage 1.

Stage 1: Forward Propagation

Now that we understand the structure of a neural network, we can investigate how input *moves* through the network to become output. This process is technically called *forward propagation.*

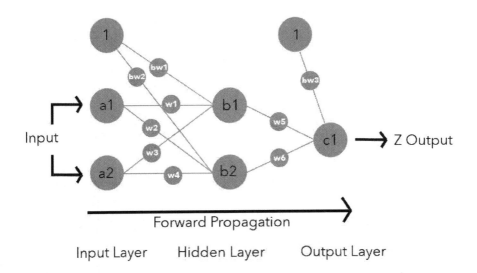

When input is passed into the network, it moves from one layer to the next until it passes through the output layer. A total of two mathematical functions are repeatedly used to make all of this possible, and we will examine both in this chapter.

This stage is organized into three parts.
1. Understanding The Mathematical Functions Used
2. Understanding Matrices
3. Fitting it All Together: Review

Ch. 5
Understanding the Mathematical Functions Used

There are a total of two mathematical functions used in this stage, and both of these functions occur *inside of* every hidden and output node. Yes, you heard right: every single node! These functions include:

- Summation operator
- Activation function

A fantastic way to understand how and where these functions operate is to view them as a *working pair* within each node:

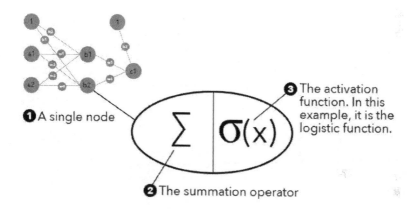

❶ A single node

❷ The summation operator

❸ The activation function. In this example, it is the logistic function.

What is a Summation Operator?

The summation operator sums a sequence of numbers, and is a convenient tool to use when dealing with large number sets and/or the repetition of an operation (such as addition or multiplication).

Within a neural network, the summation operator sums all of a node's inputs to create a *net input*. Below is the operator in its general form, followed by its specific usage for calculating the net input of a node.

General Summation Operator

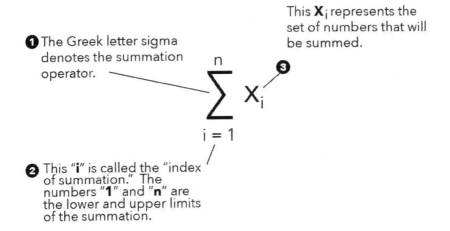

1 The Greek letter sigma denotes the summation operator.

This X_i represents the set of numbers that will be summed.

2 This "**i**" is called the "index of summation." The numbers "**1**" and "**n**" are the lower and upper limits of the summation.

$$\sum_{i=1}^{n} X_i$$

Forward Propagation: Summation Operator

When it comes to calculating the net input of a node, the summation operator looks as follows:

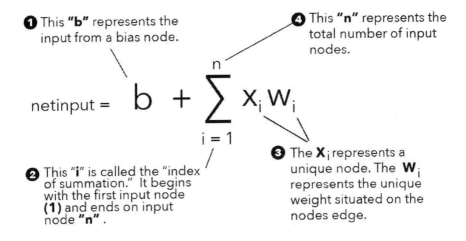

1 This "**b**" represents the input from a bias node.

4 This "**n**" represents the total number of input nodes.

$$netinput = b + \sum_{i=1}^{n} X_i W_i$$

2 This "**i**" is called the "index of summation." It begins with the first input node (**1**) and ends on input node "**n**".

3 The X_i represents a unique node. The W_i represents the unique weight situated on the nodes edge.

A Few Points to Consider :

The Bias:
The bias value is typically set to 1. Since a bias does not have an input that can alter this value, the output of a bias is always 1. This output of 1 is

then multiplied by the bias' edge weight to become input for a node. Therefore, the final output of a bias to a node is typically its edge weight value.

Input and Input Node:
The terms **"input"** and **"input node"** in this formula do not refer specifically to the net input of the network. They simply refer to the input into any hidden or output layer node. Therefore, this formula can be applied to a node in any hidden or output layer.

The summation operator is used in conjunction with matrices, and therefore an example of how this works will be given when matrices are discussed in Stage 1.

Why is a Summation Operator Used ?
Each hidden node and output node in a neural network has multiple input values. For these input values to successfully move through the network and create an output, they must be summed and turned into a *single value* when entering a new node - and this is exactly what the summation function does. To do this, the summation operator makes use of **matrices**, and its output is typically called a **dot product** or **inner product**.

What is an Activation Function?
Within a neural network, an activation function receives the output of the summation operator and transforms it into the final output of a node. On a high level, an activation function essentially "squashes" the input and transforms it into an output value that represents how much a node should contribute (i.e., how much a node should fire).

As an example, below you can see the graph of the **logistic activation function (also called Sigmoid)**, which squashes its input to create output between 0 (zero) and 1:

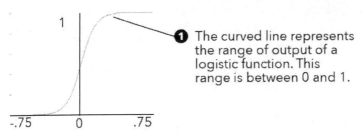

1

-.75   0   .75

1. The curved line represents the range of output of a logistic function. This range is between 0 and 1.

The equation for an activation function differs between functions. Below is the equation for the Logistic activation function that we graphed above:

$$f(x) = \frac{1}{1 + e^{-x}}$$

2. This "**x**" is the net input to a particular node.

1. This "**e**" stands for a mathematical constant that is approximately equal to 2.71828.

Types of Activation Functions

There are many types of activation functions to choose from, and a single network will often make use of multiple types. For example, a network might use the logistic function for the hidden layer nodes but use a different function for the output nodes, such as the softmax function. This is because functions differ in output, and also have unique strengths and weaknesses.

Below is a list of various activations functions. It is not an exhaustive list, but it is helpful !

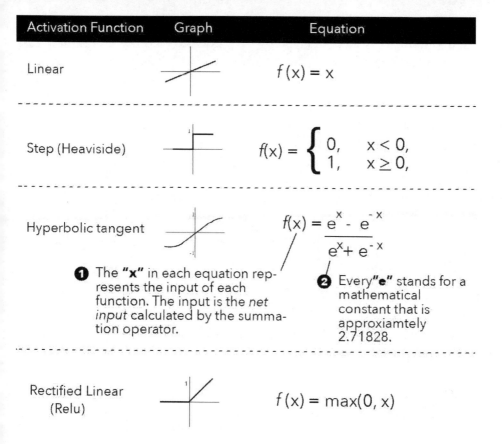

Activation Function	Graph	Equation
Linear		$f(x) = x$
Step (Heaviside)		$f(x) = \begin{cases} 0, & x < 0, \\ 1, & x \geq 0, \end{cases}$
Hyperbolic tangent		$f(x) = \dfrac{e^x - e^{-x}}{e^x + e^{-x}}$

❶ The "**x**" in each equation represents the input of each function. The input is the *net input* calculated by the summation operator.

❷ Every "**e**" stands for a mathematical constant that is approxiamtely 2.71828.

Rectified Linear (Relu)		$f(x) = max(0, x)$

Let's pause for a moment and look at the functions above.

With the **linear function**, you can see that the input *is* the output. There is no transformation that occurs. *F(x)* is simply *x*.

Now, contrast the linear function with the **step (heaviside) function**. With a step function, the output is either 0 (zero) or 1. You can see that if **x** is less than zero, the output is zero. If **x** is greater than zero or equal to zero, the output is 1. Hence, the function forms a *step* from zero to 1 when graphed.

Next, we have the **hyperbolic tangent function (tanh)**. This function is very similar to the logistic function, except that its output is between -1 and 1. This flexible range of output is exactly what enables both the logistic and tanh functions to solve nonlinear problems (we'll dive into this more below).

Finally, we come to the **rectified linear unit (ReLU)** function. With this function, all input that is <= 0 (zero) is set to 0 (zero). All input that is > 0 (zero) is equal to the input.

Why is an Activation Function Used ?

As stated above, activation functions are used to transform the output of a summation operator into the final output of a node. In recent years (2015 -) the ReLU function has gained popularity because of its phenomenal performance within deep neural networks, especially for image recognition with convolutional neural networks (CNNs).

There are multiple theories as to why its performance is superior, but no consensus has been reached.

Logistic and Hyperbolic Activation Functions

Apart from the ReLU function, the logistic and tanh functions are also popular. You will see these functions widely used in tutorials and lectures online, especially outside of CNNs.

Let's dig a bit deeper though. Why exactly are the logistic and tanh functions so popular? Here are two reasons why.

Reason #1: Introducing Non-Linearity. Neural networks are often used to solve nonlinear problems, i.e. problems that cannot be solved by separating classes with a straight line. Image classification is an excellent example of this.

An example of the importance of non-linearity can be seen below. With the image on the left, there are two groups that are being classified. These groups are easily separated with a straight line, and thus can be solved linearly.

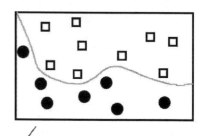

❶ There are two classes in this example. As you can see, they can be linearly divided.

❷ There are two classes in this example, but they cannot be divided linearly. Non-linearity must be introduced into the problem to successfully classify. The logistic (Sigmoid) and tanh functions both introduce this, and when used in conjunction with a multi-layer neural network can solve these problems.

Activation functions such as the tanh and logistic essentially "break" the linearity of a network and enable it to solve more complex problems. This act of breaking is an essential component that enables networks to *map* the input of a network to the output of a network and successfully train.

Reason #2: Limiting output. The tanh and logistic functions limit the output of a node to a certain range.

Ranges:
1. The Hyperbolic Tangent function produces output between -1 and 1.
2. The Logistic function produces output between 0 and 1.

There are numerous benefits to limiting output over these ranges, and one of the most significant is weight adjustment.

As you saw earlier in the activation function chart , both the logistic and tanh functions are curved. This curve, or smoothness, represents the type of output that either function can produce. On a practical level, the smoothness enables small changes in the weights and bias to produce a small change in the output.

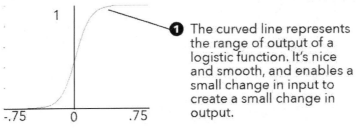

1 The curved line represents the range of output of a logistic function. It's nice and smooth, and enables a small change in input to create a small change in output.

You can view this as fine tuning that makes the task of "learning" much smoother and easier.

Now, take a moment and contrast this with the **step function**, which is...for lack of a better explanation, similar to a step.

1 The **bolded** step represents the range of output for a Step (Heaviside) function. All output is either 0 (zero) or 1. A small change in input can create a large change in output.

The step function produces an output of either 1 or 0, but nothing in-between those numbers. This means that a small change in a weight or bias is not reflected by a small change in output. Instead, the output might possibly switch from 0 (zero) to 1, or vice versa. There is no range, and this can make learning difficult!

Ch. 6
Understanding Matrices: A Brief Overview

Forward propagation is a repetitive task that requires repeated calculation using the functions we introduced above. Imagine calculating the input and output for a large network with hundreds or thousands of nodes - and by hand! The amount of time this would entail is ridiculous and impractical. Plus, the likelihood of an error would be extremely high. No thanks!

Matrices provide us with a tidy, fast and extremely useful shortcut for calculating large amounts of data in both forward and backpropagation. This section will touch on both uses, although backpropagation will be discussed further in Stage 3 and onward.

In reality, pushing matrix multiplication to its limits is one of the reasons why neural networks are powerful and useful. So let's take a moment to understand them!

What is a Matrix ?

A matrix is a rectangular array of numbers written between two square brackets. On a very high level, this can be thought of as the rows and columns in a spreadsheet. For example, the illustration below contains two dimensions - 2 rows and 4 columns, and would be labelled as a "2 by 4" matrix.

A 2 by 4 Matrix ☆

File   Edit   View   Insert   Format   Data   Tools   Add-ons   H

🖨 ↶ ↷ 🖌 $ % .0 .00 123 ▾   Arial   ▾   10

fx

	A	B	C	D
1	90	85	92	97
2	100	77	67	81
3				
4				
5				

On a technical level, a matrix is a two-dimensional array. An array is a one-dimensional list of data that can include numbers, strings etc. What's more, each element in the list is assigned a position *within* the list.

For example:

Now, one of the items in the array above *can actually be an array -* basically an array of arrays, and this is what a matrix is.

For example:

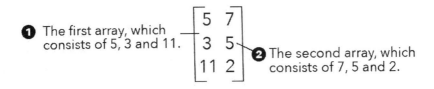

How Are The Entries in a Matrix Referenced ?

The entries in a matrix are typically referred to using numbers that denote the row and column. It's fairly straightforward.

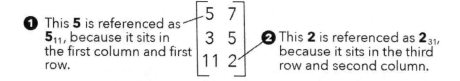

1 This **5** is referenced as 5_{11}, because it sits in the first column and first row.

2 This **2** is referenced as 2_{31}, because it sits in the third row and second column.

For example, in the above matrix the top lefthand **5** would be referenced as 5_{11} because it sits in the first row and first column. Likewise, the **2** would be referenced as 2_{31} because it sits in the third row and second column. As a whole, this matrix would be referred to as a 3 x 2 matrix, since it is 3 rows by 2 columns.

What Type of Data Does a Matrix Contain?

Think of all the information that flows through a network - both forwards and backwards. This information is stored in either a vector or matrix as it moves throughout the network.

Information stored in a matrix:
- Weights

Information stored in a vector:
- Input features
- Node inputs
- Node outputs
- Network error (which essentially is a list of weight gradients)
- Biases

How Are Matrices Used?

Matrices are used for every major calculation in both forward and backpropagation. To illustrate this, we will analyze how inputs are moved to the first hidden layer.

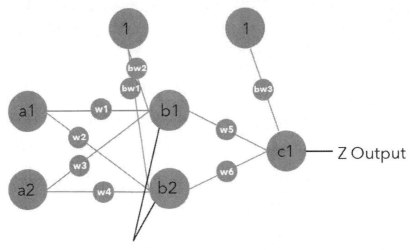

❶ To calculate the net input of **b1** and **b2**, we need to multiply **a1** and **a2** by their respective weights and then sum the answers into **b1** and **b2**, respectively. The bias also needs to be added.

To calculate the input into nodes **b1** and **b2**, we need to multiply all of the inputs into each node by their respective weights. This includes the bias value. For this to happen, the network input (which is a vector) is multiplied by the matrix of weight values that sits between *it* and the hidden layer.

To make this clearer, below is another visual example. The example is greatly simplified and should make this concept easier to grasp.

In the example above, the input vector would be multiplied by the weight matrix and the result would be added to a bias to create a new *vector* - which would be the net input to **node b1.** Let's perform this calculation below.

❶ The net input to node b1 (**b1net**), is calculated by multiplying the circled elements in the vector and matrix. The bias is also added.

To calculate **b1net** (the input to node b1), we simply need to multiply each output from **a1** and **a2** by their respective weights and then add the bias. Remember, the bias **B** is the result of the bias value multiplied by its corresponding edge weight.

Notice that we *always begin* at the top of the vector and move *horizontally* across each row in the matrix. By doing this, we multiply each element in the vector by each element in a *single* matrix row. Take a look back at the network layout above if this is not clear.

If we wrote this out:

b1net = (a1 * w1) + (a2 * w3) + bias

To clarify, the bias is arrived at by multiplying the bias value * bias weight. Thus, the above can be broken down even further:

b1net = (a1 * w1) + (a2 * w3) + (bias * bw1)

And since the bias value is typically **"1"**, this can be finalized as:

b1net = (a1 * w1) + (a2 * w3) + (1 * bw1)

The exact same process is followed for calculating the net input for b2.

❶ The net input to node b2 (**b2net**), is calculated by multiplying the circled elements in the vector and matrix. The bias is also added.

And written out:

b2net = (a1 * w2) + (a2 * w4) + bias

Again, the above can be pulled apart further to demonstrate how the bias is arrived at:

b2net = (a1 * w2) + (a2 * w4) + (1 * bw2)

Ch. 7
Fitting it All Together: A Review

In this stage we learned about how input is moved through a network to become output. Each input node is called a *feature*, and together, all features are stored in a *vector*. The information within the vector is moved through the network using two mathematical functions: the summation operator and activation function.

The summation operator sums all of the inputs into a node to create the *net input*. The activation function takes the *net input* and creates the final output of the node. Both mathematical functions occur within every hidden layer node and output layer node.

We also learned that matrix and vector multiplication are used to speed the entire process up and reduce errors.

Big Picture
Below is an illustration that highlights the *big picture* of this stage. Moving from left to right, you can see the following:

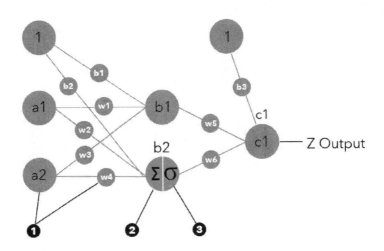

Step 1: Each input is multiplied by a weight as it travels over an *edge* (connecting line) to a node in a following layer.

Step 2: All inputs to a node, including the bias, are summed using the *summation operator*. The result is called the *total net input*.

Step 3: The *total net input* is then fed into an *activation function*, which transforms the net input into a new output. This new output is then sent out over one or more edges and multiplied by a weight, and the cycle continues until the output layer calculations are completed.

Stage 2: Calculating The Total Error

Things are looking good! We have successfully moved our input through the neural network. Our next step is to compute the *total error* of the network, which will enable the network to adjust its weights and *learn*. The total error is the difference between a network's *actual output* and *target output*.

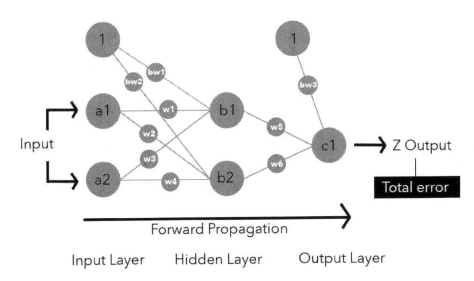

In supervised learning, each input has a corresponding target output, and this target output is what the network is aiming to replicate. In the example below, the image of a chicken has a target vector that the network will compare with the network's actual output - and any difference is labelled as the network's *total error*.

The process of matching the actual output to the target output is technically called *mapping*, and we will learn more about this moving forward. A single mathematical function is used to calculate the total error.

This stage is organized into three parts:
1. Forward
2. Understanding The Mathematical Functions Used
3. Fitting it All Together: Review

Part 1: Forward

Depending on where the network is in the training process, this stage could be the final stage. It will, however, *always be the final stage for any network that successfully trains.*

Once this stage is completed and the total error is calculated, two things can happen:

1. The network has successfully converged, ie., it has reached an acceptable low error and reached a *global minimum* or an acceptable *local minimum* that is close enough to the *global minimum*. At this point, the network ceases training.
2. The network has failed to converge. In this case, a *minimum* has not been discovered, and the network continues on to Stage 3 and continues to train. This process repeats itself until the network has converged.

Part 2: Mathematical Functions

There is a single mathematical function used in this stage, and it is only used once during forward propagation when it is applied to the output of a neural network.

- Cost Function (also referred to as a *loss function or error function*)

What is a Cost Function?

Within a neural network, a cost function transforms everything that occurs within the network into a number that represents the *total error* of the network. Essentially, it is a measure of how *wrong* a network is. On a more technical level, it maps an event or values of one or more variables onto a real number. This real number represents a "cost" or "loss" associated with the event or values.

Types of Cost Functions

There are many types of cost functions to choose from. Popular options include the Mean Squared Error, Squared Error, Root Mean Square Error and Sum of Square Errors (reasons for this will be elaborated on in the next sub-section). Other cost functions include Cross-Entropy, Exponential, Hellinger Distance, and the Kullback–Leibler Divergence.

We won't dive into every cost function, but let's pause to examine the first three.

1.Mean Squared Error (MSE).

The Mean Squared Error function takes the sum of all squared output errors in a network and averages them. In other words, the MSE measures the difference between the target output and actual output of training examples in a network.

1.The MSE equation is as follows

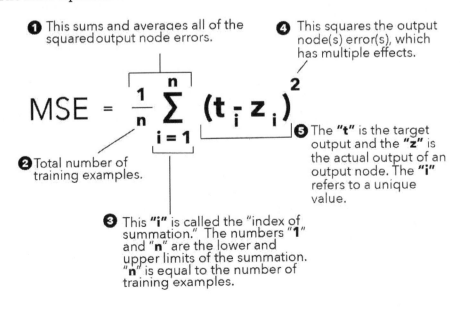

❶ This sums and averages all of the squared output node errors.

❹ This squares the output node(s) error(s), which has multiple effects.

$$MSE = \frac{1}{n} \sum_{i=1}^{n} (t_i - z_i)^2$$

❷ Total number of training examples.

❺ The "t" is the target output and the "z" is the actual output of an output node. The "i" refers to a unique value.

❸ This "i" is called the "index of summation." The numbers "1" and "n" are the lower and upper limits of the summation. "n" is equal to the number of training examples.

2. Squared Error (SE)

The Squared Error function is identical to the MSE except it is multiplied by ½, not 1/n.

$$SE = \frac{1}{2} \sum_{i=1}^{n} (t_i - z_i)^2$$

3. Root Mean Square (RMS)

The Root Mean Square performs the same calculations as the MSE, with the only difference being that it squares the answer.

The RMS equation is as follows. *Note: Elements are not labelled because they are the exact same as in the MSE equation.*

$$RMS = \sqrt{\frac{1}{n} \sum_{i=1}^{n} (t_i - z_i)^2}$$

4. The Sum of Square Errors (SSE)

The SSE function is also similar to the MSE, with the only difference being that the answer is not averaged by n number of training examples. *Note: Elements are not labelled because they are the exact same as in the MSE equation.*

$$SSE = \sum_{i=1}^{n} (t_i - z_i)^2$$

Why is a Cost Function Used ?

In order for a neural network to successfully train it must minimize the difference between its *actual output* and *target output* to find the *global minimum* (or a local minimum that is close enough to the global). This difference is the *total error*, which essentially tells us how wrong a network is. A cost function provides the *total error* - or difference - between the *target output* and *actual output*.

A Step-by-Step Breakdown: Mean Squared Error (MSE)

Calculating the total error using the Mean Squared Error (MSE) is accomplished by following 4 steps. Demonstrating the MSE will give you an idea of how the SE, RMS and SSE are also calculated.

1. Calculate the *local error* of each output node

$$(t_i - z_i)^2$$

In order to find the *total error*, the *local error* of each training example must first be calculated. Technically, the local error is the difference between a single training example's *actual output* and *target output*.

However....if there are multiple output layer nodes, this means there are multiple actual and target outputs. Hence, the local error is calculated for each node and the results are summed to create the *final local error* for a single training example. If there is only a single output node summing is not required.

Yes, this is somewhat confusing! To help clarify we have included a simple example below.

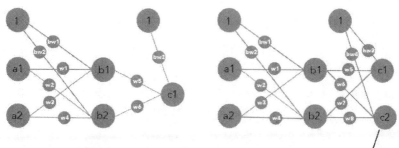

Single Node Output   Multiple Node Outputs

❶ In this example there are multiple outputs. Therefore,
the local error of each output is calculated,
and the results are summed to create a final
local error.

In the image above, the network on the left has a single output node, and
therefore only a single local error to calculate. Once calculated, this single
local error becomes the *final local error* of the training example. The
image below is an excellent example of how a single *local error* is
calculated.

❶ The actual output minus the
target output.

$$(5\text{-}1)^2$$

However, the network on the right has multiple outputs. Therefore, there
are two *local errors* to calculate. Once calculated, these local errors are
summed to become the *final local error* of the training example. See
below as an example:

$$(5\text{-}1)^2$$ ❶ The local error of **node c1**.

$$(3\text{-}2)^2$$ ❷ The local error of **node c2**.

2. Square each *local error*

$$(t_i - z_i)^2$$

This action is applied to the local error of every training example (as you can see in the above calculations). Squaring has multiple effects and its benefits are contested! We will cover two effects, the first of which is a fact, and the second which is a contested benefit.

First, the act of squaring means that the difference calculated in Step 1 is treated the same whether it is positive or negative (any number squared, even negative, automatically becomes positive). This is important because it helps the network find a *global minimum* (or a local minimum that is close enough to the global) and also keeps different signs from cancelling each other out, which can lead to a misrepresentation of how wrong the network is.

Second, squaring also helps the network converge faster. Larger derivatives are emphasised for large errors, which helps the network converge faster by taking large steps toward the global minimum. In contrast, smaller derivatives are emphasized for small errors, which helps the network converge faster by taking smaller steps towards the global minimum.

3. Sum the local errors of all training examples

$$\sum_{i=1}^{n}$$

In this step all of the *final local errors* of every training example are summed. If there is only a single training example (as in our mini scenario above) there is no need to sum. Be aware: the **n** in this equation represents training examples, *not individual nodes as in forward propagation*.

4. Multiply and Average!

$$\frac{1}{n}$$

In this final step, 1 is divided by the total number of training examples, **n**. The result is then multiplied against the sum of all local errors (Step 3). This normalizes the sum, which transforms the error into a common frame of reference that we can understand and work with.

Again, if there is only a single training example (as in our mini scenario), there is no need to divide and multiply, since the answer will be 1.

The result of steps 1-4 is the mean squared error, or *total error*. That's it!

Part 3: Fitting it All Together: Review

In this stage we learned about the *cost function*, also commonly called the *loss function*. The cost function calculates the *total error* of a network, which is the difference between the network's actual output and target output. The goal of training a network is to reduce this error to an acceptable level, close to the *global minimum*.

Big Picture

Building on the mathematical functions introduced in Stage 1, the following is a high-level view of everything we have learned so far. To keep things simple, we will begin at node **b2**, which is where we left off in Stage 1: Fitting it All Together.

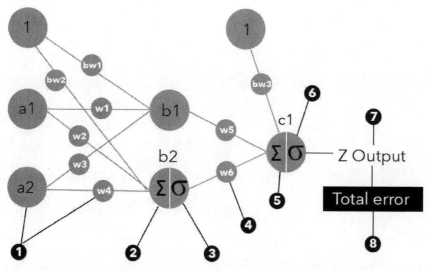

This means we are starting in-between Steps 3 and 4 (as highlighted below).

Step 3-4: The output of **b2** is multiplied by weight **w6**.
Step 5: The result is summed with all other inputs to create the net input of node c, **netc**.
Step 6: **Netc** becomes the input of an activation function.
Step 7: The activation function's output is the *final output of the network*.
Step 8: A cost function is applied to the *output of the network*, and a *total error* is calculated.

Stage 3: Calculate The Gradients

In the last chapter we calculated the *total error* of the network. Now, we are going to discover how this error is spread across every weight in the network so that we can adjust the weights to minimize the error. To do this, we are going to calculate the error of every weight in the network.

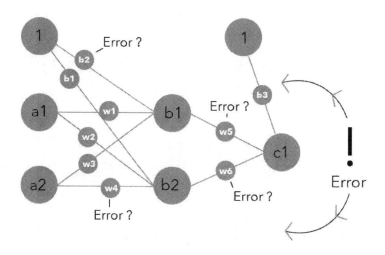

The error of a weight is technically its analytical gradient, and we will use the chain rule to calculate this. Once calculated, the network will work hard to minimize these errors and thus minimize the *total error*. This stage marks the beginning of what is technically called *backpropagation*, also referred to as a *backward pass* or simply *backprop*.

This stage is organized into four sections:

1. Understanding The Mathematical Functions Used
2. Understanding Why Gradients Are Important
3. Learning How To Calculate Gradients
4. Fitting It All Together: Review

Ch. 9
Understanding the Mathematical Functions Used

There are a total of two mathematical functions used in this stage. These functions are used together to calculate the gradient of every weight in a neural network.

- Partial derivative
- Chain Rule

What is a Partial Derivative ?

A partial derivative is best defined by beginning with the definition of a derivative. In mathematics, a derivative represents the rate of change of a function at a single point. Within neural networks this function works with real numbers (any number), which means that the *single point* mentioned above is the slope of the tangent line at a point on a graph.

That is a mouthful, so let's unpack it below with a simple illustration:

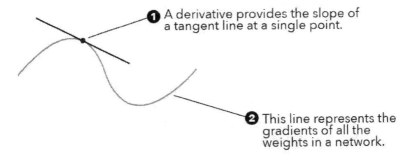

1 A derivative provides the slope of a tangent line at a single point.

2 This line represents the gradients of all the weights in a network.

A partial derivative is the derivative of a function which has two or more variables *but with respect to only one variable*. What's more, all the other variables are treated as constant. In other words, a partial derivative enables you to measure how a single variable (out of many) impacts another single variable. Take for example the black elements in the neural network below.

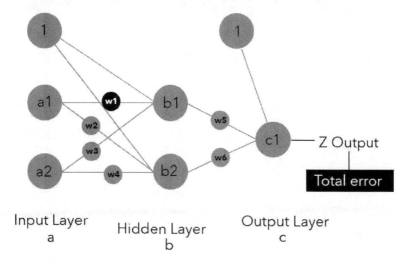

Input Layer
a

Hidden Layer
b

Output Layer
c

The partial derivative allows us to discover how a change in weight **w1** affects the **total error** - while all the other weights remain constant. The same can be calculated for **w2, w3, bw1, bw2 etc.**

The partial derivative is often written using "lower delta y over lower delta x" (meaning the *difference* in y divided by the *difference* in x. To continue with our example above, measuring a change in the **total error** by a change in the weight **w1** would look as follows:

❶ The partial derivative of the **total error**.

$$\frac{\partial E}{\partial W_1}$$

❷ The partial derivative of weight **W1.**

Why is a partial derivative used ?

To update the weights of a neural network we need to know how much a change in a *specific* weight affects the *total error*. That is, we want to find the rate of change between two variables: a specific *weight* and the *total error*. This might seem easy enough, but it poses a problem that can be outlined as follows:

1. There are multiple connected variables (weights, node outputs, node inputs) within a network. *Note: within neural networks variables are often called parameters. Parameter is the correct technical term to use, but we have chosen to use variable for its simplicity.*

2. A slight change in a single weight will affect all variables that occur after it within the network. The larger the network, the greater the impact of a change.
3. Given the ramification of a slight change, calculating how a *specific weight* impacts the *total error* is challenging.
4. Partial derivatives are the answer to this challenge. They enable us to calculate how a function (*total error)* changes with respect to a *single* variable (*specific weight)* while keeping all other variables constant.

One last and important point: within neural networks, the partial derivative is often described as a *gradient*. This is because they are the same! We will touch on this more in Part 2.

What is the chain rule ?

The chain rule is used to find a partial derivative when an equation consists of a function *inside* another function. In other words, it is used to differentiate the function of another function. We will explain this more in depth further on when calculating partial derivatives. For now, here is what the chain rule looks like:

$$\frac{\partial z}{\partial x} = \frac{\partial z}{\partial y} \cdot \frac{\partial y}{\partial x}$$

Why is the chain rule used ?

The best way to answer this is to work from a high-level downwards.

Discovering the error of a specific weight is an important aspect of training a network. In order to discover a weight's error, its partial derivative is calculated. In order to calculate the partial derivative, the chain rule is used multiple times. And that - in a nutshell - is why the chain rule is used.

Ch. 10
Understanding Why Gradient Are Important

Gradients are extremely important and in many ways form the backbone of how a neural network is trained. Let's discover why this is.

What is a gradient?
Within the context of a neural network, a gradient is the following:

- A gradient is the slope of the *local error* for a specific weight. In other words, it is the individual error of a specific weight and it tells us how much a change in a specific weight affects the *total error*.

- A gradient is derived by calculating the partial derivative of a specific weight. In other words, a gradient is a partial derivative. This is very important to understand and cannot be overstated!

When graphed, this is what a gradient looks like. Look familiar ?

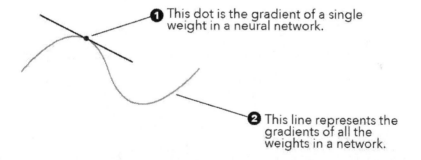

1 This dot is the gradient of a single weight in a neural network.

2 This line represents the gradients of all the weights in a network.

Alright. That's fantastic. Let's pull back the curtain even more to get a better understanding.

Gradient importance: in-depth explanation
The goal of this stage is to calculate the gradients for each weight, but why is this important? Let's step back for a minute to answer this question. Training a network involves minimizing the difference between *actual output* and *target output*. This difference is called the *total error* and was

discovered in Stage 2 by using a *cost function*. The question is, once we have discovered the *total error,* what elements can we adjust to minimize it ?

The output of a network is a product of two elements: network input and weights. The input is fixed, so to minimize the *total error* our only option is to adjust the weights. This fact raises a second question that we must answer: how much do we adjust each weight ? Do we increase the weight or decrease the weight?

In other words, what is the exact combination of weights that will produce a minimal *total error* (technically called a *global minimum*) ?

Our answer is *gradient descent,* which is an optimization method that helps us find the exact combination of weights and ultimately discover a *global minimum.*

This, however, raises a third and final question: how do we perform gradient descent?

To perform gradient descent we must calculate the partial derivatives of each weight and then *use the partial derivatives to update each weight.* There are a few ways this can be approached and each has its own pros and cons. Each method, however, has the same goal and begins by calculating partial derivatives. We will explore gradient descent and its various approaches in Stage 5.

Now, back to calculating partial derivatives! When calculating partial derivatives, it is important to realize that there are two different types of weights:

- Weights on the inside of the network situated between input/hidden nodes.
- Weights on the outside of the network situated between a hidden node and output node.

Below is an illustration to help clarify each type:

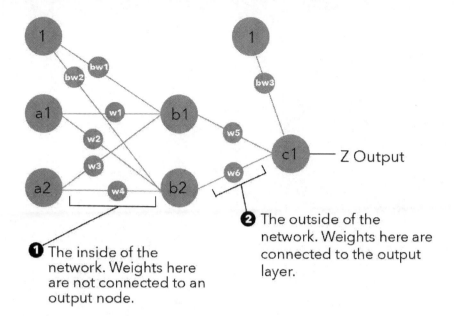

1 The inside of the network. Weights here are not connected to an output node.

2 The outside of the network. Weights here are connected to the output layer.

Now, why is this important? The fact is, each type of weight requires a slightly different method for calculating the partial derivative. What's more, the partial derivatives for output layer weights are *always* calculated *first* because their values are used to calculate the interior partial derivatives.

Let's move on and start calculating the gradients.

Gradient Calculation

The gradient of a weight is the partial derivative of the respective weight. Calculating the partial derivative of an output layer weight and hidden layer weight consists of a number of steps, and each is somewhat different. The same applies to calculating the partial derivatives of bias weights.

This section is organized into the following parts:
1. Calculating The Partial Derivative of Output Layer Weights
2. Calculating The Partial Derivative of Output Layer Bias Weights
3. Calculating The Partial Derivative of Hidden Layer Weights
4. Calculating The Partial Derivative of Hidden Layer Bias Weights

Please remember: the notation you will see is 100% changeable. We have chosen our notation for ease of use and simplicity.

Ch. 11
Calculating the Partial Derivative of Output Layer Weights

This part is divided into the following steps:

Step 1. Discovering The Formula
Step 2. Unpacking The Formula
Step 3. Calculating The Partial Derivatives
Step 4. Compacting The Formula

Step 1/4: Discovering The Formula

The formula below is used to calculate the partial derivative of either a hidden layer or output layer weight. Note what each element stands for.

❶ Partial derivative symbol.

❸ This "E" represents the total error of the network. It could be any other letter or number, but "E" is intuitive.

$$\frac{\partial E}{\partial W_5}$$

❷ This "W" represents weight. It could be any other letter or number, but "W" is intuitive.

❹ This "5" represents a specific weight that falls between the "b" and "c" layers. This is the weight we are finding the partial derivative for.

What does this all mean ? Technically the formula is read as: the partial derivative of the *total error* with respect to **w5.** In layman's terms it asks the question: How much does a change in weight **5** affect the *total error* ?

Now, seeing the above is helpful, but what is it *actually* solving for ? The image below helps answer this question with a visual twist. Note the following:

- The elements in **black** are what we are concerned with. Essentially, we want to know how much a change in weight **5** affects the **total error**.
- Remember from Stage 2: The **total error** is computed by applying a *cost function* to the output **z.**

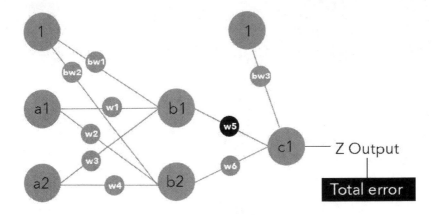

Step 2/4: Unpacking the Formula

The formula above is helpful, but what do we plug into it ? How do we go solve it ? In order to find our answer the formula needs to be unpacked. This is because there are multiple partial derivatives *inside of it,* and to find our answer, we need to unpack all partial derivatives involved.

In other words, **W5** is connected through a series of *partial derivatives* to the **total error.** You can picture this as follows. *Note: the black dots are for multiplication.*

$$\frac{\partial E}{\partial W_5} = \boxed{?} \longrightarrow \bullet \longrightarrow \boxed{?} \longrightarrow \bullet \longrightarrow \boxed{?} \Rightarrow \text{Total Error}$$

Each of these partial derivatives explains how a certain variable, if changed, affects the variable after it. To put it another way, each partial derivative asks the question: how much does a change in _____ affect _____ ?

To eventually solve our question we need to unpack every single partial derivative, solve each derivative, and multiply the answers together. Our final answer will tell us how a change in weight **w5** affects the **total error.**

The question is, how do we do this? Our answer is the **chain rule**, which helps us quickly unpack partial derivatives. As we apply the chain rule, and for sake of ease, we will label these partial derivatives as *intermediate variables*. This will make it easier for us to distinguish what we are discussing, and is also somewhat intuitive.

First unpacking:

Let's apply the chain rule and unpack our first derivative.

On a high level, working backwards from the **total error,** we can see that there are two *intermediate variables* to be concerned with. First, we need to know how much a change in the output **z** affects the **total error.** Second, we need to know how much a change in weight **w5** affects the output **z**. This constitutes our first unpacking, as you can see below.

❶ The partial derivative of the **total error** with respect to the output **Z**.

$$\frac{\partial E}{\partial W_5} = \frac{\partial E}{\partial Z} \frac{\partial Z}{\partial W_5}$$

❷ The partial derivative of the output **Z** with respect to weight **w5.**

Perfect. As you can see, we have *unpacked* the partial derivative on the left with two partial derivatives on the right. By doing this we have applied the chain rule. However, we can't stop here!

Let's zoom in and unpack the illustration from above.

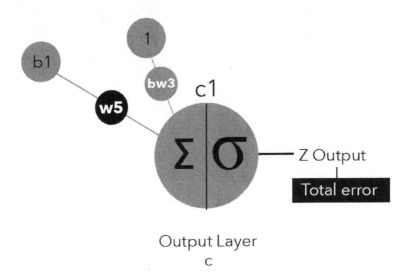

Output Layer
c

As you can see, the output node **c1** is divided into two sections. On the left is the **summation operator** which sums the **net input** into the node. On the right is the **logistic activation function**, which takes the output of the summation operator and applies a function to it before passing it out as the final output **z**.

Second unpacking:

If we pause for a moment, we can see that the partial derivative on the far right of our equation is not fully unpacked. Initially, we thought it went directly from **z** to **w5**, but now we see differently. The fact is, there is still another *intermediate variable* inside of it which tells us how the net input into the node **c1** affects **z** . So, we will apply the **chain rule** to the far right partial derivative and expand it even further.

$$\frac{\partial Z}{\partial W_5} = \frac{\partial Z}{\partial Znet_c} \frac{\partial Znet_c}{\partial W_5}$$

Voila! We are now finished unpacking all of the partial derivatives. Now, once we put everything together our new equation is:

① The partial derivative of the total error with respect to the output **Z**.

③ The partial derivative of **netc** with respect to weight **w5.**.

$$\frac{\partial E}{\partial W_5} = \frac{\partial E}{\partial Z} \frac{\partial Z}{\partial net_c} \frac{\partial net_c}{\partial W_5}$$

② The partial derivative of **Z** with respect to **netc.**

Finally! Do you see the pattern above ? Our answer is essentially a chain of partial derivatives multiplied together. *Note that the denominator always becomes the numerator for the next partial derivative! This is what links the above together and creates a chain, or a zipper-like structure.*

Step 3/4: Calculating The Partial Derivatives
Our next step is to calculate the partial derivatives, and this is where your calculus needs to shine! We will not be going into great depth for each, but simply summarizing how it is discovered. Working from the left of the equation to the right:

Derivative 1:

$$\frac{\partial E}{\partial Z}$$

This partial derivative is asking the question *how much does a change in z affect the **total error** ?* To answer this we need to look at the cost function formula, which occurs in between z and **total error.** To minimize distraction, here is the cost function formula stripped down with no explanations.

$$MSE = \frac{1}{n} \sum_{i=1}^{n} (t_i - z_i)^2$$

By looking at the *cost function* formula, we can see that the partial derivative is **the negative of the target output - actual output.** Therefore:

❶ This **"t"** represents the target output of a particular node.

$$\frac{\partial E}{\partial Z} = -(t - z)$$

❷ This **"z"** represents the actual output of a particular node.

However, for sake of clarity the negatives are often cancelled out.

$$\frac{\partial E}{\partial Z} = (z - t)$$

Derivative 2:

$$\frac{\partial Z}{\partial net_c}$$

This partial derivative is asking the question *how much does a change in* ***netc*** *affect z?* To answer this we need to look at the *activation function* formula, which occurs in-between **netc** and **z.** Here is the logistic *activation function* formula stripped down with no explanations.

$$f(x) = \frac{1}{1 + e^{-x}}$$

Without going into detail, the answer is found below. It is the derivative of the activation function:

$$\frac{\partial Z}{\partial net_c} = z(1 - z)$$

❶ Each "**z**" represents the actual output of a particular node.

Derivative 3:

$$\frac{\partial net_c}{\partial W_5}$$

This partial derivative is asking the question *how much does a change in w5 affect netc?*

By looking at the zoomed in illustration, we can see that **netc** is equal to the output of **b1** multiplied by **w5**. This tells us that the answer is the output of **b1**. For sake of clarity we will label the output of b1 as **outb1.**

$$\frac{\partial net_c}{\partial W_5} = out_{b1}$$

Finally! Now that we have calculated all the derivatives we have our full equation. This equation is used to find the partial derivative of any output layer weight. Note the following:

- **(z - t)** and **z(1-t)** remain the same for any output layer weight you are calculating for.
- The variables **w5** and **outb1** will change depending on the weight you are calculating for.

❶ Derivative 1   **❸** Derivative 3

$$\frac{\partial E}{\partial W_5} = (z\text{-}t)\, z(1 - z)\, out_{b1}$$

❷ Derivative 2

Step 4: Compacting The Formula

Many view the above equation as somewhat clunky and not optimal. In light of this, you will often see the formula compacted even further.

$$\frac{\partial E}{\partial W_5} = \delta_z \text{out}_{b1}$$

1 This δ_z is the node delta for the output layer. See below for further explanation.

2 This represents the output of the node **b1**.

What is Delta$_z$? Delta$_z$ is the *node delta*, and it is a term that conveniently sums up 99% of the terms in the full equation. Technically, it is the derivative of **c1's** activation function multiplied by the difference between the *actual output* and *target output*. Here it is unpacked:

$$\delta_z = (z\text{-}t)\, z(1 - z)$$

Ch. 12
Calculating the Partial Derivative of Output Layer Bias Weights

This part is divided into two sections:

1. It is already calculated
2. Beware: Different Delta$_z$'s

It is Already Calculated

The partial derivative of a hidden node bias weight is very easy to calculate! In fact, we have already calculated it above. It is Delta$_z$!

$$\delta_z = (z\text{-}t)\, z(1 - z)$$

Therefore, if we applied this to the **bw3** weight in our example neural network, it would look as follows:

$$\frac{\partial E}{\partial B_{w3}} = (z\text{-}t)\, z(1 - z)$$

With the above, we are asking the question: *how much does a change in* **bw3** *affect the* ***total error?*** The answer is our **node delta** that we calculated previously in Part 1. Now, you may be wondering, why is there no **outb1** as in the example below ?

$$\frac{\partial E}{\partial W_5} = \delta_z \, \text{out}_{b1}$$

❶ This δ_z is the node delta for the output layer. See below for further explanation.

❷ This represents the output of the node **b1**.

The fact is, a bias is not connected to a previous layer and therefore does not have an input. Therefore, we are left with the node delta as the partial derivative of any weight in the output layer.

Beware: Different Delta$_z$'s!

The current example we are using only has a single output node; however, if there are multiple output nodes, the Delta$_z$ changes depending on the partial derivative being calculated! If the incorrect Delta$_z$ is used the partial derivative will be wrong.

To demonstrate this we have included a new network layout below with two output nodes. By looking at it, we can see that **bw3** is connected to **node c1,** while **bw4** is connected to **node c2.**

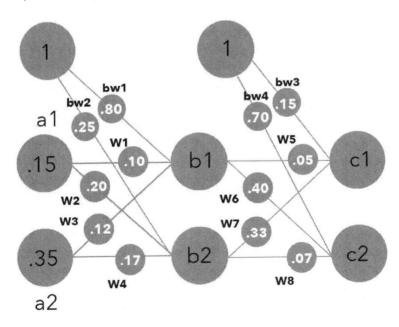

In light of this, **bw3** would make use of the Delta$_z$ for **node c1**, while **bw4** would use the Delta$_z$ for **node c2.**

Ch. 13
Calculating the Partial Derivative of Hidden Layer Weights

Calculating the partial derivative of a hidden layer weight is very similar to that of an output layer weight. In fact, there isn't much difference apart from the level of complexity introduced.

On a high level, we use the same initial formula as above and unpack it using the chain rule.

Let's dig in. This section is divided into the following steps:

Step 1. Discovering the formula
Step 2. Unpacking The Formula
Step 3. Calculating The Partial Derivatives
Step 4. Compacting The Formula

Step 1: Discovering The Formula

The formula below is used to calculate the partial derivative of either a hidden layer node or output layer node. Note the slight difference between this formula and the previous formula for hidden layer weights: in this formula our focus is on **w1**.

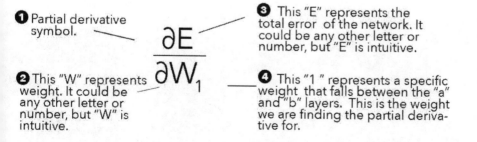

❶ Partial derivative symbol.

❸ This "E" represents the total error of the network. It could be any other letter or number, but "E" is intuitive.

$$\frac{\partial E}{\partial W_1}$$

❷ This "W" represents weight. It could be any other letter or number, but "W" is intuitive.

❹ This "1 " represents a specific weight that falls between the "a" and "b" layers. This is the weight we are finding the partial derivative for.

The question we are trying to solve is: How much does a change in **w1** affect the **total error** ? You can see this visually below.

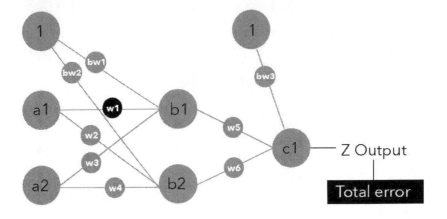

Step 2: Unpacking The Formula

To calculate the partial derivative of **w1** we need to work backwards from the output **Z** to **w1** and compute the partial derivatives of all *intermediate variables*. This is where the complexity of calculating an answer begins to emerge. As you can see above, we are now dealing with a weight that is deeper within the network and therefore affects more variables.

To calculate our answer we must use the chain rule multiple times to unpack lots of partial derivatives - and the more complex a network is, the more difficult this becomes.

As we did before, let's take a closer look at the *edges* we are concerned with to find out exactly what we need to do.

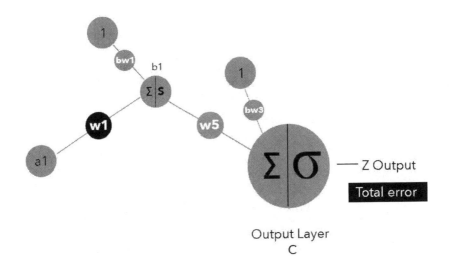

Output Layer
C

⬆️ First unpacking:

To start let's focus on the area from *a1 to w5*. When we do this, we can see there are at least two *intermediate variables* to be concerned with. The first is how much a change in the net input of b1 - **netb1** - affects the **total error**. The second is how much a change in weight **w1** affects **netb1**. To clarify, **netb1** is the summation of all inputs into node **b1**. This constitutes our first unpacking, as you can see below.

❶ The partial derivative of the **total error** with respect to **netb1**.

$$\frac{\partial E}{\partial W_1} = \frac{\partial E}{\partial net_{b1}} \frac{\partial net_{b1}}{\partial W_1}$$

❷ The partial derivative of **netb1** with respect to weight **w1**.

⬆️ Second unpacking:

Fantastic. We have now officially used the chain rule and are off to a good start. Our second step is to determine if the partial derivatives we just unpacked can *themselves* be unpacked. Lucky for us, only the first one needs our attention! By looking at the network layout, we can unpack the first partial derivative as follows by applying the chain rule again:

$$\frac{\partial E}{\partial net_{b1}} = \frac{\partial E}{\partial net_{c1}} \frac{\partial net_{c1}}{\partial net_{b1}}$$

Our second unpacking is now complete. However, the partial derivative on the far right *itself* can be unpacked further. Let's use the chain rule one last time.

⬆️ Third unpacking:

$$\frac{\partial net_{c1}}{\partial net_{b1}} = \frac{\partial net_{c1}}{\partial out_{b1}} \frac{\partial out_{b1}}{\partial net_{b1}}$$

We have completed all of our unpacking. Phew! Our formula is now the following. *Note that the numbers above each partial derivative will be used for solving each derivative.*

$$\frac{\partial E}{\partial W_1} = \overset{\text{❶}}{\frac{\partial E}{\partial net_{c1}}} \overset{\text{❷}}{\frac{\partial net_{c1}}{\partial out_{b1}}} \overset{\text{❸}}{\frac{\partial out_{b1}}{\partial net_{b1}}} \overset{\text{❹}}{\frac{\partial net_{b1}}{\partial W_1}}$$

Step 3: Solving The Derivatives

Our next step is to solve each derivative. We will solve each of the partial derivatives above working from left to right. To help us do this we'll paste in the network image once again. No need to skip back a few pages!

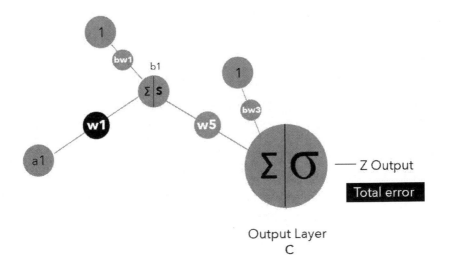

Output Layer
C

Derivative #1

$$\frac{\partial E}{\partial net_{c1}}$$

This partial derivative is asking the question: *how much does a change in **netc1** affect the **total error**?* We have already computed this derivative when we calculated the partial derivative of an output layer weight. When we calculated this before, we labelled it as Deltaz.

$$\frac{\partial E}{\partial net_{c1}} = \delta_z$$

$$\delta_z = (z-t)\, z(1 - z)$$

However, before this derivative is solved we must clarify an important point: by changing **netc1**, we impact the net input of *all output nodes* in layer **c.** To reiterate with slightly different language, if we adjust the input to **b1** we impact the input of all nodes in layer **c.**

In light of this, our final partial derivative includes the summation operator. Although the example we are using to demonstrate derivative calculations only contains a single output node, neural networks often contain multiple output nodes.

Therefore, when working with multiple output nodes, the Delta$_z$ for each output node is calculated and all results are summed together.

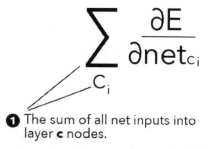

❶ The sum of all net inputs into layer **c** nodes.

For example, if our network example contained two output nodes, the following would be summed together. *Note: the inclusion of w_1 and w_2 will be explained when calculating derivative # 2 below.*

$$\sum_C \begin{array}{l} \delta_{z1} = (z\text{-}t)\, z(1 - z)\, w_1 \\[8pt] \delta_{z2} = (z\text{-}t)\, z(1 - z)\, w_2 \end{array}$$

Combining everything we have done, and for the sake of clarity, we will now label this as the following. *Note that this contains the answer to our partial derivative.*

$$\sum_C \delta_z$$

Derivative #2

$$\frac{\partial net_{c1}}{\partial out_{b1}}$$

This partial derivative is asking the question: *how much does a change in* **out_{b1}** *affect* **net_{c1}**? By looking at the network layout, and recalling that the derivative of a constant times the variable is the constant, we can see that the answer is **w5.**

$$\frac{\partial net_{c1}}{\partial out_{b1}} = W_5$$

Here is an important fact: if a network has multiple output nodes, this partial derivative (**w5** in this case) would be multiplied by each Delta$_z$. For example, if a network has two output nodes and two hidden nodes, the following would be calculated. *Note:* **W_1** *and* **W_2** *represent output* *layer weights that are affected by the change made to a single weight in the hidden layer.*

$$\sum_C \begin{array}{l} \delta_{z1} = (z\text{-}t)\; z(1-z)\; w_1 \\[1em] \delta_{z2} = (z\text{-}t)\; z(1-z)\; w_2 \end{array}$$

Derivative #3

$$\frac{\partial out_{b1}}{\partial net_{b1}}$$

This partial derivative is asking the question: *how much does a change in* **net b1** *affect* **out b1**? To answer this we need to look at the *activation function* formula, which occurs in between **netb1** and **outb1**. Here is the *logistic activation function* formula stripped down with no explanations.

$$f(x) = \frac{1}{1 + e^{-x}}$$

Without going into detail, the answer is found below. It is essentially the derivative of the activation function:

$$\frac{\partial out_{b1}}{\partial net_{b1}} = out_{b1}(1 - out_{b1})$$

Derivative #4

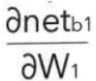

$$\frac{\partial net_{b1}}{\partial W_1}$$

This partial derivative is asking the question: *how much does a change in w1 affect netb1?*

By looking at the network illustration, we can see that the answer is the output of **a1**. For sake of clarity, we will label this as **outa1**.

$$\frac{\partial net_{b1}}{\partial W_1} = out_{a1}$$

At last! Now that we have calculated all the derivatives, we have our full equation. Let's put the equation together.

① Derivative 1   **③** Derivative 3

$$\frac{\partial E}{\partial W_1} = \left(\sum_c \delta_z \ W_5 \right) out_{b1} \left(1 - out_{b1} \right) out_{a1}$$

② Derivative 2   **④** Derivative 4

Step 4: Compacting The Formula

The above formula is often compacted to make it easier to work with.

① This δ represents the layered delta for the node **b1**.

$$\frac{\partial E}{\partial Z} = \delta_b \ out_{a1}$$

② This represents the output of the node **a1**.

What is Delta$_b$? Delta$_b$ is the *node delta*, which is an expression that conveniently sums up 99% of the terms in the full equation. Technically, it is the difference between the *actual output* and *target output* of all nodes in layer **c**, multiplied by **w5**, multiplied by the derivative of node **b1's** activation function. Here it is unpacked:

$$\delta_b = \left(\sum_c \delta_z W_5 \right) out_{b1} \left(1 - out_{b1} \right)$$

Ch. 14
Calculating the Partial Derivative of Hidden Layer Bias Weights

This part is divided into two sections:
1. It is Already Calculated
2. Beware: Different Delta$_b$'s !

It is Already Calculated

The partial derivative of a hidden layer bias weight is very similar to an output layer weight. And yes - we have already calculated it! It is the previous layer's node delta, Delta$_b$.

$$\delta_b = \left(\sum_c \delta_z W_i \right) \text{out}_i (1 - \text{out}_i)$$

❶ All of the letter **"i"'s** refer to a unique value. This value depends on the gradient we are calculating.

Therefore, if we were to apply this to our example network for **bw1**, it would look as follows:

$$\frac{\partial E}{\partial B_{w1}} = \left(\sum_c \delta_z W_5 \right) \text{out}_{b1} (1 - \text{out}_{b1})$$

With the above, we are asking the question: *how much does a change in* **bw1** *affect the* ***total error?*** The answer is our **node delta** that we calculated above in Part 3. Again, you may be wondering, why is there no **out$_{a1}$** as in the example below ?

$$\frac{\partial E}{\partial Z} = \delta_b \, out_{a1}$$

❶ This δ represents the layered delta for the node **b1**.

❷ This represents the output of the node **a1**.

Our answer is the same as when we calculated the output layer weight bias - a bias is not connected to a previous layer and therefore does not have an input. Therefore, we are left with the node delta of a previous layer as the partial derivative of any weight in a hidden layer.

Beware: Different Delta$_b$'s!

$\square_b$ changes depending on the partial derivative you are calculating for! This is true for both hidden layers and output layers.

To demonstrate this, we have included an additional network layout below. By looking at it, we can see that **bw1** is connected to **node b1**, while **bw2** is connected to **node b2**. In light of this, **bw1** would make use of node **b1's** Delta$_b$. , while **bw2** would make use of **node b2's** Delta$_b$. *Note: this will be expanded with an example in Part 3.*

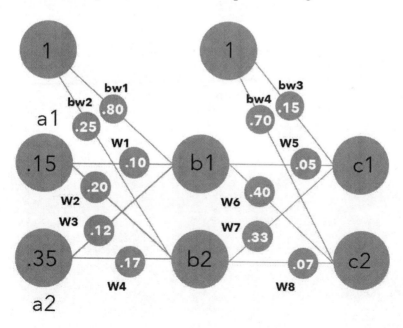

Ch. 15
Fitting it All Together: A Review

This is a very complex stage! However, on a high-level we have learned how to calculate the *gradient* of a weight, which is technically a *partial derivative*. All of the gradients combined create the *total error,* which is computed using a *cost function.*

There are two types of weights: those that are connected to an output node, and those that are not. Calculating the partial derivative for each is a slightly different process. Plus, we learned that the same is true for calculating the partial derivatives of bias weights.

Building on the mathematical functions introduced in Stages 1 and 2, the following is a high-level view of everything we have learned so far. We will begin at the *total error,* which is where we left off in Stage 2: Fitting it All Together. This means we will begin at Step 9, and we will also end there, because it is the only step.

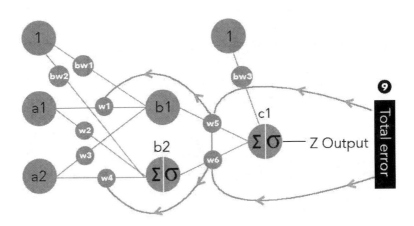

Step 9: As you can see above, the *total error* calculated by the cost function is propagated back through the entire network. What this means is that the *total error* is essentially broken up and distributed back through the network to *every single weight.* The question is, how much of the error should each weight receive ?

This is accomplished by calculating the *partial derivative* for each weight. Remember, the partial derivative asks: How much does a change in a specific weight affect the *total error* ? By calculating the partial derivative of each weight, the network decides how much of the *total error* every weight should receive.

For sake of clarity, in the example above we have removed the former steps (1-8), and placed the *total error* on its side. Please note: the example is very *simple* and not all backpropagation links are shown.

Stage 4: Checking the Gradients

The goal of Stage 4 is to check if the analytical gradient calculations made in Stage 3 are approximately accurate. Many might consider this stage to be optional, and it certainly is; however, gradient checking is very important (especially with deep neural networks), which is why we have opted to include it.

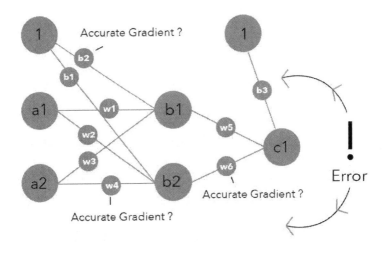

Gradient checking is a very simple procedure that enables the analytical gradients we just calculated to be *manually checked* for accuracy. This is accomplished by using a *numerical estimate* of the partial derivatives - which might sound complex, but it is quite straightforward. Once a gradient has been successfully checked, gradient checking is disabled.

This stage is organized into four sections:

1. Understanding Numerical Estimation
2. Discovering The Formula
3. Calculating The Numerical Estimation
4. Fitting it All Together: Review

Ch. 16
Understanding Numerical Estimation

Deriving all the gradients (partial derivatives) of a neural network is *a lot of* computation, and the more calculations that occur, the greater the probability of an error. Numerical estimation is a fantastic tool that can help minimize these errors. On a high level, numerical estimation essentially checks an analytical gradient against an estimated gradient, and if the value is close to the backpropagation version of the gradient, it passes!

Numerical estimation of the gradient works by creating *two points* to either side of some point on the error curve drawn out by varying a single weight. The slope between those two points is the gradient with respect to that weight, which is shown below:

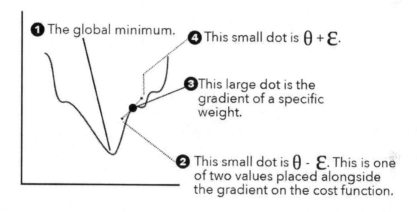

❶ The global minimum.

❹ This small dot is $\theta + \varepsilon$.

❸ This large dot is the gradient of a specific weight.

❷ This small dot is $\theta - \varepsilon$. This is one of two values placed alongside the gradient on the cost function.

In the image above, the gradient of the weight that we are checking is at the large dot, while the small dots on either side of it are the two points we mentioned previously. As you can see, each point consists of a calculation that has two parts: The first is a vector of all the weights in a network, which we call the Greek letter Theta. The second is a small preset number (a hyperparameter), usually denoted by the Greek letter Epsilon.

$$\theta$$
Theta

$$\varepsilon$$
Epsilon

Theta

Theta can be a little tricky to understand because it is actually *two things*:

- It is a vector that contains all of the weights in a network, but...
- It also represents a single, specific weight in a network.

Although Theta is a vector that contains all the weights in a network, in this specific calculation it represents a *single weight* within the network. The weight it represents contains the gradient that we are manually checking, and Epsilon is only added to this weight. If this is confusing, don't worry! It will be expanded on below with an example.

Epsilon

Epsilon is a very small value that is subtracted or added to a weight's gradient to create the *two points* on either side of the gradient. A common value for Epsilon is 10^{-4} (0.0001) or 10^{-5} (0.00001).

Calculating The Numerical Estimate

The numerical estimation is derived by calculating the slope of the two points mentioned above, which can be calculated by using rise over run. Visually, this can be shown as follows:

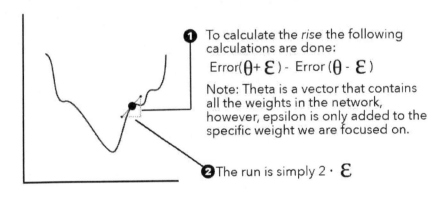

1 To calculate the *rise* the following calculations are done:

$$Error(\theta + \varepsilon) - Error(\theta - \varepsilon)$$

Note: Theta is a vector that contains all the weights in the network, however, epsilon is only added to the specific weight we are focused on.

2 The run is simply $2 \cdot \varepsilon$

Ch. 17
Discovering the Formula

The formula to calculate the numerical estimate of the gradient of a single weight is below. To tie this back to Section 1, the formula is simply *rise divided by run*.

❶ The Greek letter Theta is a vector that contains all the weights in the network, but don't be mistaken! The Epsilon value is only added to single weight at a time. See below for more details.

$$\frac{\text{Error}(\theta + \mathcal{E}) - \text{Error}(\theta - \mathcal{E})}{2 \cdot \mathcal{E}}$$

❷ Epsilon represents a very small number. In this case it is 10^{-4}.

Calculating the Numerical Estimation

There are 7 steps to calculate and assess the numerical estimate. To help us move through these, we'll break the formula into two parts and calculate them in order.

We'll use an arbitrary weight, **w5,** to illustrate some of the calculations.

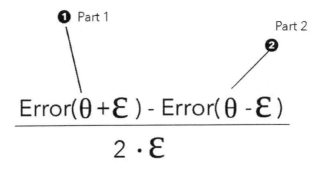

$$\frac{\text{Error}(\theta + \varepsilon) - \text{Error}(\theta - \varepsilon)}{2 \cdot \varepsilon}$$

Part 1:

Step 1. Add Epsilon

To start, we add the Epsilon value to the weight we are checking the gradient for. For example, if we are checking the gradient of weight 5, w5, we add epsilon to this to create a new w5 value.

$$W5_{new} = W5 + \varepsilon$$

Step 2. Recalculate The Total Error Of The Network

Next, we recalculate the total error of the network using the value we calculated in Step 1. For example, if we recalculated the value of weight 5, **w5,** we would use this new value instead of the old **w5** value when making our calculations. This means we would work again through Stages 1-2.

This is somewhat challenging to show with an illustration, but on a high level it can be viewed as the following:

$$\text{Error}(\theta + \varepsilon) = \text{Error}(W1, W2, W3, W4, W5 + \varepsilon)$$

Note that the Greek letter Theta is a vector that holds all the weights in a network, but that Epsilon is only added to the weight we are checking the gradient for.

We now have the following part of our formula:

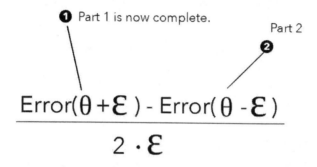

1 Part 1 is now complete.

Part 2

2

$$\frac{\text{Error}(\theta + \varepsilon) - \text{Error}(\theta - \varepsilon)}{2 \cdot \varepsilon}$$

Part 2

Step 3. Subtract Epsilon

Moving forward, we recalculate the total error again but this time we subtract the Epsilon value from the weight we are concerned with. Continuing with our example, this means we would subtract Epsilon from **w5.**

$$W5_{new} = W5 - \varepsilon$$

Step 4. Recalculate The Total Error Of The Network

Finally, we recalculate the total error of the network by using the value we calculated in Step 3. This means we would work again through Stages 1-2.

$$\text{Error}(\theta - \varepsilon) = \text{Error}(W1, W2, W3, W4, W5 - \varepsilon)$$

We have now completed the formula:

Part 1 is now complete.

Part 2 is now complete.

$$\frac{\text{Error}(\theta + \varepsilon) - \text{Error}(\theta - \varepsilon)}{2 \cdot \varepsilon}$$

Step 5: Calculate The Numerical Approximation

Now that we have our entire formula, we can calculate the numerical approximation for the weight we are concerned with. To do this, the formula that we have completed is worked out.

Step 6: Measure Against the Analytic Gradient

Next, we check the numerical approximation against the analytical gradient. Doing this will tell us how "far off" the two gradients are from each other. If you recall, the analytical gradient is the original gradient that the network computed.

Difference = Analytical Gradient - Numerical Gradient

To make the output value easier to work with and interpret, you should convert it to scientific notation. For example:

$$
\begin{aligned}
\textbf{Difference} &= \text{Analytical Gradient - Numerical Gradient} \\
&= 0.000246 - 0.00024599 \\
&= 0.00000001 \\
&= 10^{-8}
\end{aligned}
$$

Step 7: Compute The Relative Error

The output from Step 6 is likely *very small* and thus difficult to interpret. Is it good? Bad? Ok? To help bring clarity, a common practice is to compute the Relative Error and check it against a table of relative errors. The relative error is calculated by dividing the difference by whichever is larger. You can see this below:

$$\text{Relative Error} = \frac{\text{Analytical Gradient - Numerical Gradient}}{\text{max(Analytical Gradient, Numerical Gradient)}}$$

$$= \frac{\text{Difference}}{\text{max(Analytical Gradient, Numerical Gradient)}}$$

The result is converted to scientific notation and then checked against a table of relative error rules of thumb, such as the table below. The goal, of course, is for the numerical gradient to be as close to the analytical gradient as possible, i.e., for the relative error to be as minimal as possible.

Relative Error	Rules of Thumb
$> 10^{-2}$	High chance the gradient is wrong.
$< 10^{-2}$ and $> 10^{-4}$	A double red flag. Something is wrong.
Between 10^{-5} and 10^{-6}	A single red flag. Use caution.
$<= 10^{-7}$	High chance the gradient is correct.

Ch. 19
Fitting it All Together: A Review

In this stage, we covered gradient checking, which is a method that can be used to manually check a computed gradient and make sure it is (more or less) accurate. Gradient checking is optional, but many well-known researchers and scientists within the machine learning field advocate for it.

We learned that gradients are manually checked by creating two fictitious points on either side of a computed gradient, and then calculating the slope of those points - which is rise over run. The result of this is the *numerical estimation* of the gradient, which is then subtracted from the original computed gradient, called the *analytical* gradient.

The end result is the difference between the estimated gradient and the computed gradient, but this difference is often very small, such as 10^{-8}. To make this number more useful, it is often converted to a *relative error* and then checked against a relative error guide, or table.

If the relative error is small enough to be acceptable, the computed gradient is considered valid and passes the test.

Stage 5: Updating the Weights

The goal of Stage 5 is to update the weights in a neural network. This is accomplished by continuing to apply the *backpropagation* we began in Stage 3 *by using* the gradients we calculated in Stage 3 through an optimization process known as *gradient descent*. That's a mouthful - but don't worry, we will unpack it all below.

This stage is organized into four sections:
1. What is Gradient Descent ?
2. Methods of Gradient Descent
3. Updating the Weights
4. Fitting it All Together: Review

Ch. 20
What is Gradient Descent?

Gradient descent is an optimization method that helps us find the exact combination of weights for a network that will minimize the output error. It is how we *turn the dials* on our network and fine tune it so that we are satisfied with its output. A good way to approach gradient descent is simply by unpacking its name. Let's start there!

- *Gradient* essentially means slope.
- *Descent* means to descend, or go down.
- Therefore, *gradient descent* has something to do with descending down a slope.

Perfect. This now raises a few questions:

- What are we descending ?
- What is the slope ?
- How fast do we descend ?

With *gradient descent,* we descend down the slope of gradients to find the *lowest point,* which is where the *error* is smallest. Remember, the gradients are the errors of the individual weights, and the goal of a network is to minimize these errors. By descending down the gradients we are actively trying to minimize the *cost function* and arrive at the *global minimum.*

Our steps are determined by the steepness of the slope (the gradient itself) and the *learning rate.*

The learning rate is a value that speeds up or slows down how quickly an algorithm learns. Technically, it is a hyperparameter set in the pre-stage that determines the size of step an algorithm takes when moving towards a *global minimum.*

Most study cases you will find online make use of learning rates between 0.0001 and 1. You can read more on the learning rate in our extended definitions section.

Back to gradient descent. To give an intuitive explanation of how gradient descent *works* and its *goal*, many textbooks use the analogy of a person hiking down a mountain. It is quite helpful, so we have decided to include it. *Note that the goal is, of course, to reach the bottom where the global minimum lies.*

2 This is the hiker who is hiking down the hill. He is headed towards the global minimum at the bottom of the hill.

Total Error

W   **1** The global minimum.

Do you see a potential problem though ? The above is a simple representation that does not take into consideration the complexity of *real-life* neural networks. In practice, neural networks have *hundreds* if not *thousands* of weights which completely change the landscape of the simple graph above.

In fact, what if the terrain the hiker was descending is not smooth, but has many *local minima* that he can become stuck in and falsely believe is the *global minimum* ? See the example below. Again, it is extremely simplified.

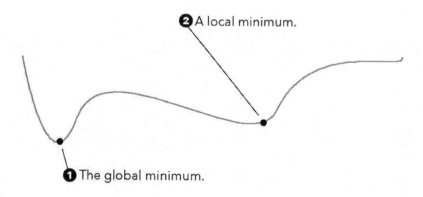

2 A local minimum.

1 The global minimum.

This is a potential pitfall that all neural networks face when using gradient descent. It also reflects the reality of the world we live in and the data we collect as input: it's messy, imperfect, and hard to work with. So, what can we do? To help mitigate the problem an optimization algorithm is typically used in conjunction with back propagation.

A popular example is *Momentum*, which is used to help push the algorithm out of a *local minimum*. It essentially adds a boost to the direction the network is moving in. *Momentum* does not always work, but it is a popular technique often used with the backpropagation algorithm. Alongside the *learning rate, momentum* is preset for the algorithm in Stage 1.

Other optimization methods include the *Nesterov accelerated gradient* (which fine tunes *momentum*), *Adagrad, Adadelta (Adagrad extension), RMSprop, and Adam.*

Ch. 21
Gradient Descent Methods

This section is divided into the following parts:
1. Introduction
2. Batch Gradient Descent
3. Stochastic Gradient Descent (SGD)
4. Mini-Batch Gradient Descent

Introduction

In Stage 3, we calculated all of the partial derivatives for every weight in the network. Now we can update these weights using gradient descent. There are a number of different approaches to implementing gradient descent, and remember: matrix multiplication is used in each to compute the gradients! You can skip back to Stage 3 to review matrix multiplication if necessary.

On a high level, the methods differ with regards to how much data is used before a weight is adjusted. Each method has its own pros and cons as well as advocates, but practically speaking, the significant tradeoffs include time and accuracy.

Here is an interesting fact: networks will often make use of two or more methods to achieve the *global minimum* (although not at the same time; only a single method can be used at one time). For example, a network might begin training using SGD, and then switch to Batch once the noise created by SGD begins to interfere with convergence. There are many strategies and theories on how to select the best method, but those are beyond this introductory text.

Below is a very brief explanation of three gradient descent methods:

Batch Gradient Descent (also called Full-Batch)

Full-Batch training works by summing the gradients for every training set element and then updating the weights. This updating is technically one iteration (also called an epoch). For example, if a training set consists of 10,000 images, by definition it also contains 10,000 elements. With this example, an update of the weights will not occur until after the gradients of all 10,000 images have been calculated and combined.

As you can imagine, this type of training can be very slow. Unlike SGD however (see below), Batch training is guaranteed to find a local minimum on a non-convex surface and *global minimum* on a convex surface. See below for an example of convex vs non-convex.

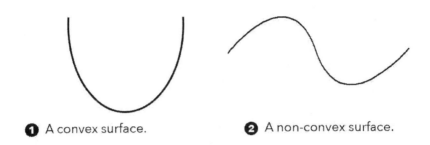

1 A convex surface.   **2** A non-convex surface.

Stochastic Gradient Descent (also called SGD / Online)

With SGD, the weights in a network are modified after *every training set element*. What this means is that a *single* training set element is used to update a parameter (weight) in a particular iteration. For example, if a training set consists of 10,000 images, each image is a training set element (and all examples combined to form a training set).

With SGD, it is important to note that the training set is shuffled because the order of the data can cause the network to become biased. There are various approaches to shuffling, such as a single shuffle at the beginning of training or after every epoch.

SGD is typically faster than full-batch training, especially early on in the training process. However, it can also produce much more noise, which causes the network to bounce around near the *global minimum* but never reach it.

Mini-Batch Gradient Descent

Mini-Batch training works by summing the gradients for multiple training set elements (but not all of them) and then updating the weights. The size of the mini-batch can be preset as a hyperparameter or randomly chosen by the algorithm.To continue with our example above, these elements would be n number of images from our training set of 10,000 images.

Mini-Batch falls somewhere in between Full-Batch and SGD, and has been used very successfully with neural networks. It also tends to be one of the most popular gradient descent methods.

Ch. 22
Updating Weights

Updating the weights of a neural network is quite straightforward, at least compared to computing the gradients! *Note that updating bias weights is no different than updating any other weight. The exact same formula is used.*

This section is divided into the following parts:
1. General Weight Update Equation
2. Batch Training Weight Update Equation
3. SGD Training Weight Update Equation
4. Mini-Batch Training Weight Update Equation

General Weight Update Equation

The general equation for updating a weight is given below. Note that the equation is slightly altered depending on the gradient descent method used. These alterations will be explored further on.

Remember, the big idea is to continue applying this update rule so that the algorithm can *descend* the gradients and minimize the cost function. The weight update formula does this by taking a step in the *opposite direction* of a weight's gradient. See below.

Note: For the equations below we have continued using the notation from previous examples.

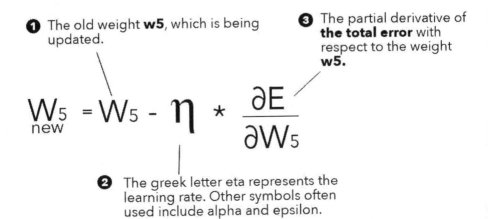

❶ The old weight **w5**, which is being updated.

❸ The partial derivative of **the total error** with respect to the weight **w5.**

$$W_{5_{new}} = W_5 - \eta * \frac{\partial E}{\partial W_5}$$

❷ The greek letter eta represents the learning rate. Other symbols often used include alpha and epsilon.

New weight = old weight - learning rate x the partial derivative of the *total error* with respect to weight **w5** .

Working from right to left, what we are doing is multiplying the error (which is the partial derivative) by the learning rate and subtracting that from the current weight we are focused on. As a result, we are basically cancelling out that weight's contribution to the error.

Big Picture Reading
The whole idea behind gradient descent is to minimize the error of every single weight in a neural network, which results in the *total error* of the network being minimized. In the equation above, the **subtraction** operation is what enables this to happen!

The error of the current weight is *subtracted from the current weight* **w5**. This is what enables the network to take a step *down the slope* and minimize the weight's error. To help speed this up or slow it down, it is multiplied by a *learning rate*.

Batch Training Weight Update Equation
For batch training, the weights are updated after passing an entire training set through the network; that is, after one epoch has been completed. The following equation is used:

❶ This represents a weight that is being updated. The Greek letter Theta θ is often used in this context and represents a vector. The **W** denotes a specific weight within the vector.

❹ This E(θ) is used to represent the cost function of all weights in the network.

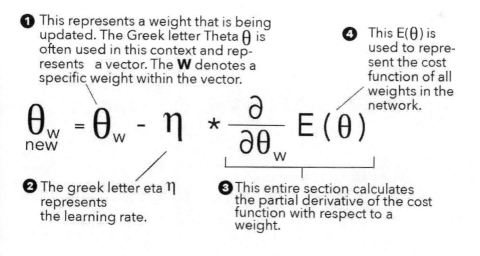

$$\theta_{w}^{new} = \theta_{w} - \eta * \frac{\partial}{\partial\theta_{w}} E(\theta)$$

❷ The greek letter eta η represents the learning rate.

❸ This entire section calculates the partial derivative of the cost function with respect to a weight.

Technical Reading: Left to Right
New weight = old weight - learning rate multiplied by the partial derivative of the *total error* with respect to a weight, **w.**

Working from right to left, what we are doing is multiplying the error (which is the partial derivative) of a weight by the learning rate and subtracting that from the current weight we are focused on.

Big Picture Reading
The purpose of a weight update is to minimize the error of a weight and help move the network towards minimizing the *total error*.

Now, this formula makes use of the Greek letter **Theta** and letter **w.**
Theta is a vector that contains all of the weights in the network, while **w** is used to denote a specific weight *within* the vector.
Theta can be pictured as a line that contains all the weights in a network:

To understand this further, let's unpack the far right side of the batch training equation. In the equation above this is labelled as **#3.**

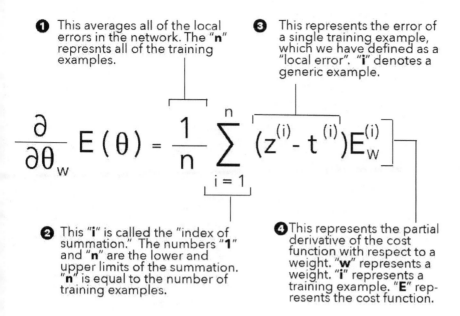

① This averages all of the local errors in the network. The "**n**" represnts all of the training examples.

③ This represents the error of a single training example, which we have defined as a "local error". "**i**" denotes a generic example.

$$\frac{\partial}{\partial \theta_w} E(\theta) = \frac{1}{n} \sum_{i=1}^{n} (z^{(i)} - t^{(i)}) E_w^{(i)}$$

② This "**i**" is called the "index of summation." The numbers "**1**" and "**n**" are the lower and upper limits of the summation. "**n**" is equal to the number of training examples.

④ This represents the partial derivative of the cost function with respect to a weight. "**w**" represents a weight. "**i**" represents a training example. "**E**" represents the cost function.

As you can see above, batch training makes use of the average sum of all the training example errors in a network. Note: **z - t** is the *actual output - target output*.

SGD Training Weight Update Equation

For SGD training, the weights are updated after each training set element is passed through the network. This approach uses the same equation as the general equation given at the top of this section. Here is the equation again:

① The old weight **w5**, which is being updated.

③ The partial derivative of **the total error** with respect to the weight **w5.**

$$W_{5_{new}} = W_5 - \eta * \frac{\partial E}{\partial W_5}$$

② The greek letter eta represents the learning rate. Other symbols often used include alpha and epsilon.

New weight = old weight - learning rate multiplied by the partial derivative of the *total error* with respect to a weight, **w.**

Working from right to left, what we are doing is multiplying the error (which is the partial derivative) of a weight by the learning rate and subtracting that from the current weight we are focused on.

Big Picture Reading
With SGD, weights are updated after each single training example is passed through the network. This is why the equation above does not use the summation operator as in batch training.

Mini-Batch Training Weight Update Equation

For mini-batch training the weights are updated after a certain number of training elements have passed through the network. In the equation below, the batch size is set to 10 training examples.

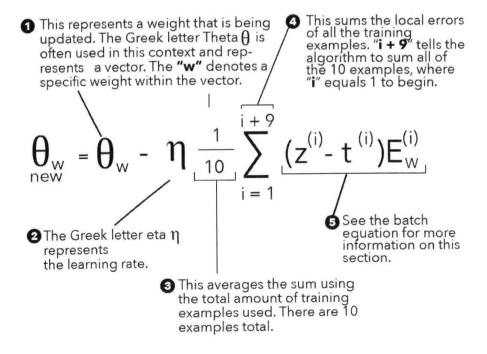

❶ This represents a weight that is being updated. The Greek letter Theta θ is often used in this context and represents a vector. The **"w"** denotes a specific weight within the vector.

❹ This sums the local errors of all the training examples. "**i + 9**" tells the algorithm to sum all of the 10 examples, where "**i**" equals 1 to begin.

$$\theta_{w}^{new} = \theta_{w} - \eta \frac{1}{10} \sum_{i=1}^{i+9} (z^{(i)} - t^{(i)}) E_{w}^{(i)}$$

❷ The Greek letter eta η represents the learning rate.

❺ See the batch equation for more information on this section.

❸ This averages the sum using the total amount of training examples used. There are 10 examples total.

In this case there are a total of 10 training examples in the mini-batch.
Hypothetically, if there were 1000 training examples in the training set,
updates would occur every 10 training examples. Thus, there would be a
total of 100 weight updates.

Ch. 23
Fitting it All Together: A Review

At this stage, we have learned how the weights in a neural network are updated. At a high level, this is accomplished by moving in the opposite direction of each gradient (partial derivative), calculated in Stage 3. This process is called *gradient descent* due to the fact that the goal is to move *down* the gradients to find the lowest error.

We also learned that there are three popular methods for applying gradient descent, including Batch gradient descent, Stochastic gradient descent, and Mini-batch gradient descent. Each varies in the amount of data used to update and the time it takes to update.

Constructing a Network: Hands-On Example

In this chapter we will build a simple neural network using all the concepts and functions we learned in the previous few chapters. Our example will be basic but hopefully very intuitive. Many examples available online are either hopelessly abstract or make use of the same data sets, which can be repetitive.

Our goal is to be crystal clear and engaging, but with a touch of fun and uniqueness.

This chapter is divided into the following sections:

1. Defining the Scenario
2. Pre-Stage: Network Structure
3. Stage 1: Running Data Through the Network
4. Stage 2: Calculating the Total Error
5. Stage 3: Calculating the Gradients
6. Stage 4: Gradient Checking
7. Stage 5: Updating the Weights
8. Wrapping it All Up: Final Review

Defining the Scenario: Man vs Chicken

On a high level we are going to build a neural network that can distinguish between two 8x8 grayscale pixel characters: man or chicken. To do this we will systematically work through each of the stages we learned about in the previous chapters.

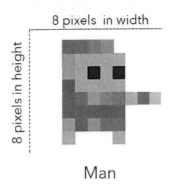

8 pixels in width

8 pixels in height

Man

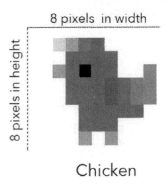

8 pixels in width

8 pixels in height

Chicken

Now, if we were to create this entire network and perform all the calculations, this example would be extremely long and repetitive - not to mention a nightmare for display on a Kindle.

With that being said, we are only going to follow one of our characters as it is broken apart and fed through the network - and in a very, VERY simplified manner. This will provide you with a good idea of how each mathematical function operates. Ready to go ? Let's dig in.

Note: Convolutional neural networks (CNN's) - and not traditional feedforward networks - are typically used for image classification. CNN's performance is superior in this regard, which is why major technology companies such as Google and Facebook use CNN's to classify images. However, images provide a fantastic visual that can help in the teaching process, which is precisely why we will be using them!

Pre-Stage: Network Structure

This stage is organized into the following sections:
1. Determining Structural Elements
2. Understanding the Input Layer
3. Understanding the Output Layer
4. Simplifying our Network
5. Stage Review

Section 1: Determining Structural Elements
In this stage we need to define a number of structural elements.

Total input nodes: 64.
This number is derived from each image, which is 8x8 pixels.

Total hidden layers: 1.
We will follow Stanford's Andrew Ng's recommendation, which is to begin with a single hidden layer.

Total hidden nodes: 64.
Again, we will follow popular opinion and use the same number of hidden nodes as input nodes. It is a good place to start.

Total output nodes: 2.
Due to the fact that we are classifying two elements we will use two output nodes. Each node will represent a unique class: man or chicken. If we pass an image of a chicken through the network, our goal is for the output node that represents the *chicken* class to output a **"1"**, and the man class output a **0 (zero)**.

Likewise, if we pass an image of a man through the network, our goal is for the output node that represents the *man* class to output a **"1"**, and the chicken class output a **0 (zero)**.

Bias value: 1.
We will set our bias' to have a value of 1. Again, this is common practice.

Weight values: Random
We will assign random values to begin.

Learning rate: 0.5
We will begin with an initial learning rate of 0.5. This number is somewhat arbitrary, and it can be changed as the network learns.

Now that we have selected all of our structural elements, let's take a look at our neural network architecture. Note that due to its size, not all nodes and weights can be shown. There are over 4200 weights in total - plus 132 nodes (including biases). In light of this, we will be working with a simplified version of our network.

However, on a grand scale our network appears as follows:

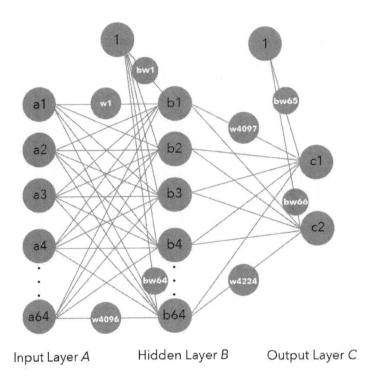

Input Layer *A*   Hidden Layer *B*   Output Layer *C*

Before we transition to a simplified version of our network it is a good idea to take a closer look at the input and output layers.

Section 2: Understanding the Input Layer
Our input layer has a total of 64 input nodes. As you can see in the chicken image below, this is because each pixel becomes a node in the input layer.

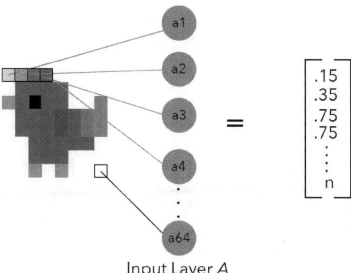

Input Layer *A*

If you remember, all input features are stored within a vector, which is also shown on the far right of the image. But what about the numbers inside the vector ? Where are they coming from? Let's zoom in once more to find our answer.

❶ This .15 represents the gray-scale value of the first pixel, which is the **a1** node in the network diagram. The pixel is a light gray, and thus the gray-scale value is approx. 0.15.

❷ This .75 represents the grayscale value of the third pixel, which is the **a3** node. The pixel is dark, but not black, so its value is 0.75.

As you can see above, the numbers in the vector represent the grayscale value of each node in the input layer. The *n* represents the grayscale value of the last input node, node 64.

Section 3: Understanding the Output Layer

The output layer has two nodes, and as we mentioned in the pre-stage, each node represents a specific class: man or chicken.

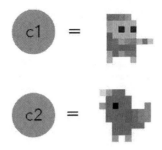

Each training image we put through the network has a target output assigned to it which is stored in a vector. In the example below, if we put an image of a chicken through the network, our target output is a vector containing 0 (zero) on the top and 1 below. The reverse is also true for an image of a man. This is technically called *one-hot encoding*.

One-hot encoding is method that transforms categorical features (such as our man and chicken) into a new format of 1's and 0 (zeros). This format is popular because it has proven to work very well with classification and regression algorithms.

With one-hot encoding, the correct target output node is "hot", i.e., 1, while the rest are 0 (zero).This is why when we pass a chicken through, we want the output to be a vector as close to the following as possible:

*Note that **0 (zero)** is the output of **node c1,** and **1** is the output of **node c2.***

Section 4: Simplifying our Network

To finish off this stage, let's take a look at the simplified version of this network we will be working with. This will require a mental leap and some imagination! What we will be doing is reducing our entire image classifying network to a handful of nodes, which makes it much easier to work with as an example, especially on a Kindle.

Specifically, we will imagine that our image can be classified using only two input nodes and two hidden nodes. To do this we will continue using the input values we introduced earlier for **a1** and **a2**. These inputs have values of 0.15 and 0.35, which should make for an interesting case study.

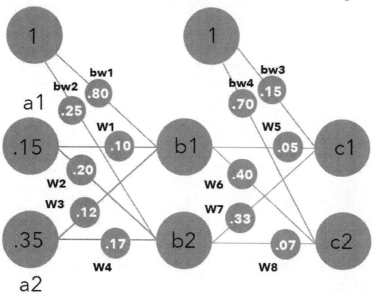

Section 5: Stage Review

In this stage we created our network structure, which includes the number of input nodes, hidden nodes/layers, output nodes, bias values, weight values, and the learning rate. We also concluded the following:

-   If the input is a man, we want the output to be a vector of [1, 0].
-   If the input is a chicken, we want the output to be [0, 1].

We also learned about how an image is broken down, pixel, by pixel, and stored within an input vector. Lastly, we simplified the structure so that it can be used for teaching purposes.

Let's move on to Stage 1 and begin to move our input through the network.

Stage 1: Running Data Through the Network

It's now time to run our input data through the network. If applicable, answers will be rounded to a maximum of four decimal places.

This stage is divided into three sections:
1. Moving From the Input Layer to the Hidden Layer
2. Moving From the Hidden Layer to the Output Layer
3. Stage Review

Section 1: Moving From the Input Layer to the Hidden Layer

Let's begin by calculating the net input to nodes **b1 and b2,** which we will label as **netb1 and netb2,** respectively.

To calculate **netb1 and netb2**, we need to sum all of the inputs into nodes **b1** and **b2**. Using the **summation operator**, here is what this would look like for **netb1.**

① "**n**" stands for total number of nodes that must be multiplied by their respective weights.

$$netb1 = \sum_{i=1}^{n} (a_i \ w_i) + bias$$

② "**a**" and "**w**" stand for the output of a node and its respective weight. The "**i**" indicates a unique value.

As we learned in Part 2: Stage 2, the above can be written as follows:

netb1 = (outa1 * w1) + (outa2 * w3) + (bias * bw1)

And when we substitute with our values, we find our answer:

netb1 = (0.15 * 0.10) + (0.35 * 0.12) + (1 * 0.80) **= 0.857**

The exact same is done for **netb2.**

netb2 = (outa1 * w2) + (outa2 * w4) + (bias * bw2)

And substitution yields our answer:

netb2 = (0.15 * 0.20) + (0.35 * 0.17) + (1 * 0.25) **= 0.3395**

Let's see how this looks within our network. Remember, each net input value will be put through an activation function before it leaves its respective node.

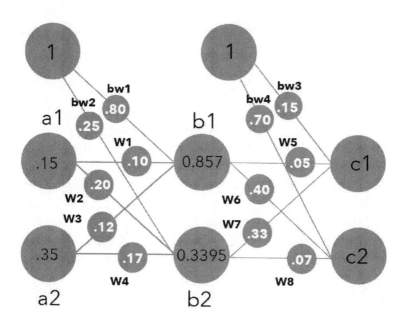

Section 2: Moving From the Hidden Layer to the Output Layer

This section is divided into the following:

1. Introduction
2. Applying B1 and B2 Activation Functions
3. Moving From Layer B to C

Introduction

To move our values from the hidden layer to the output layer, we must first apply an activation function to our net input values. This will provide us with the output for our hidden nodes, which we can then move forward along their respective edges.

Here is a picture of a node to remind you of how the summation operator and activation function work together:

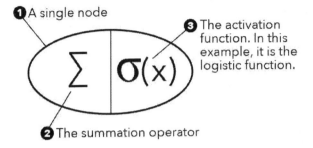

1 A single node

2 The summation operator

3 The activation function. In this example, it is the logistic function.

Applying B1 and B2 Activation Functions

Here is the Logistic activation function with highlights for **node b1**.

$$f(x) = \frac{1}{1 + e^{-x}}$$

1 This **negative x** represents the net input of b1, or **netb1**.

2 This **"e"** is a mathematical constant. Its value is approximately 2.71828.

Now, let's substitute our value for **netb1**, along with the constant **e**.

$$f(netb1) = \frac{1}{1 + 2.71828^{-0.857}}$$

$$= \frac{1}{1.424433719}$$

$$= 0.7020$$

Now, let's do the same for **netb2.**

$$f(x) = \frac{1}{1 + e^{-x}}$$

❶ This **negative x** represents the net input of b2, or **netb2**.

❷ This **"e"** is a mathematical constant. Its value is approximately 2.71828.

Substituting:

$$f(netb2) = \frac{1}{1 + 2.71828^{-0.3395}}$$

$$= \frac{1}{1.71212646}$$

$$= 0.5841$$

Fantastic! We have now calculated the outputs of nodes **b1** and **b2.** If we update the values of each hidden node, the network now looks as follows:

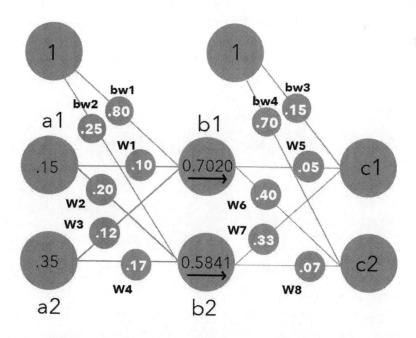

Moving From Layer B to C

All we need to do now is move this output to **nodes c1** and **c2.** To do this, we will follow the same steps as we did previously when me moved from the input layer to the hidden layer. Since we have already explained the steps involved, we will only show the calculations.

To calculate **netc1:**

netc1 = (outb1 * w5) + (outb2 * w7) + (bias * bw3)

We then substitute our values to find our answer:

netc1 = (0.7020 * 0.05) + (0.5841 * .33) + (1 * 0.15) **= 0.3779**

To calculate **netc2:**

netc2 = (outb1 * w6) + (outb2 * w8) + (bias * bw4)

Substituting:

netc2 = (0.7020 * 0.40) + (0.5841 * .07) + (1 * 0.70) **= 1.0217**

Our last step in this stage is to apply an activation function to **netc1** and **netc2.** This will provide us with the final outputs of the network. We will continue using the Logistic activation function.

$$f(netc1) = \frac{1}{1 + 2.71828^{-0.3779}}$$

$$= \frac{1}{1.685299201}$$

$$= 0.5934$$

And for **netc2:**

$$f(netc2) = \frac{1}{1 + 2.71828^{\,-1.0217}}$$

$$= \frac{1}{1.359982697}$$

$$= 0.7353$$

The final outputs for the network are **0.5934** and **0.7353**. Let's wrap up this stage with a top-down view:

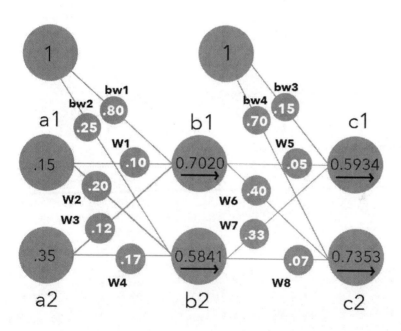

Stage Review:

In this stage we moved our input through the network to create a final output. To do this we made use of two mathematical functions: the summation operator and an activation function. Each of these functions was used twice for each node as we moved the input through the network.

We also made use of **e,** which is a mathematical constant with a value of approximately 2.71828.

Stage 2: Calculating the Total Error

It is now time to calculate the total error of the network! To do this, we will compare the actual output of the network to the target output of the network. If you recall, a target output is provided for each training example that is passed through the network. In our case, our training example is an image of a chicken, and our target output is a vector with a value of 0 (zero) for **node c1** and value of 1 for **node c2.**

With that being said, let's move forward and calculate the total error of our network. Our total error will be the combined *local error* of each output node. To calculate this, we need to apply a **cost function** to each output node. For this example, we will use the Squared Error (SE) function.

The SE formula is below. Note that we have highlighted elements for output layer c:

$$SE = \frac{1}{2} \sum_{i=1}^{n} \left(t_i - z_i \right)^2$$

To find our total error we will apply the cost function to each output node, and then sum the answers together. Since we are only concerned with a single training example there is no need to sum over all training examples, which means we will ignore the summation operator.

Calculating the Local Error of Node c1

To start, we'll substitute our values to find the local error for **node c1**.

$$SE_{c1} = (0 - 0.5934)^2$$
$$= -0.5934^2$$
$$= 0.3521$$

Calculating the Local Error of Node c2

We will follow the same steps for **node c2**.

$$SE_{c2} = (1 - 0.7353)^2$$
$$= 0.2647^2$$
$$= 0.070$$

Finally, we will sum our local errors to discover the final local error.

$$SE = 0.3521 + 0.070$$
$$= 0.4221$$

Now that we have the final local error, we can plug it into our cost function formula.

$$SE = \frac{1}{2} * 0.4221$$
$$= 0.21105$$

There we have it! **Our total error is 0.21105.** Let's see what this looks like from a high-level:

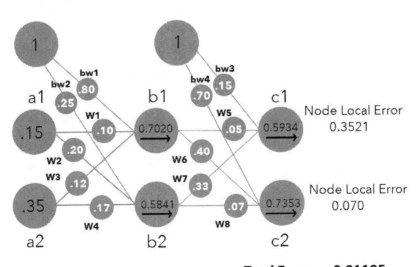

Stage Review:

This stage was quite brief. In this stage we calculated the total error of the network by applying a cost function to the actual output of the network. Since there are two outputs, we applied the cost function to each, summed the results and multiplied by 1/2 to find the total error.

Stage 3: Calculating the Gradients

Since we have successfully moved our inputs through the network and calculated our total error, we can now begin backpropagation!

Due to the above, this stage is divided into the following sections:
1. Calculating Gradients for Output Layer Weights
2. Calculating Output Layer Bias Weights
3. Calculating Gradients for Hidden Layer Weights
4. Calculating Hidden Layer Bias Weights
5. All Gradients

Section 1: Calculating Gradients For Output Layer Weights

We will begin by calculating the partial derivative for **weight w5** using the derivative formula we learned in Part 2: Stage 3. To do this we will work step-by-step through the problem, and then follow the same steps for weight **w6**. For the remaining weights we will summarize the answers. Below is a quick visual to help provide context.

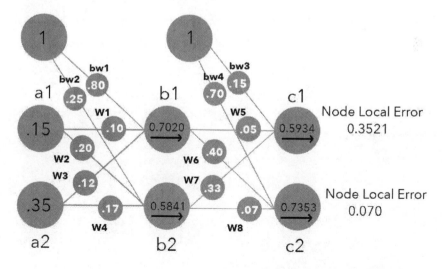

Calculating the gradient with respect to w5

The formula we will use is directly below. To refresh your memory, the formula is essentially asking the question: How much does a change in weight **w5** affect the **total error ?** Note that the "t" and "z" in the equation only apply to **node c1**. This is because **w5** only affects **node c1**. For clarification take a peek back at the network layout above!

❶ Every **"z"** in this formula is the actual output for **node c1**.

$$\frac{\partial E}{\partial W_5} = (z\text{-}t)\, z(1\text{-}z)\, out_{b1}$$

❷ This **"t"** is the target output for **node c1**.

Substituting our values, we get the following:

$$\frac{\partial E}{\partial W_5} = (0.5934 - 0) * 0.5934(1\text{-}0.5934) * 0.7020$$

$$= 0.5934 * 0.5934(0.4066) * 0.7020$$

$$= 0.1005$$

Calculating the gradient with respect to w6

The formula we will use is below. Note what changes though! The "t" and "z" in this equation only apply to **node c2**. This is because **w6** only affects **node c2**.

❶ Every **"z"** in this formula is the actual output for **node c2**.

$$\frac{\partial E}{\partial W_6} = (z\text{-}t)\, z(1\text{-}z)\, out_{b1}$$

❷ This **"t"** is the target output for **node c2**.

Substituting our values:

$$\frac{\partial E}{\partial W_6} = (0.7353 - 1) * 0.7353\,(1 - 0.7353\,) * 0.7020$$

$$= -0.2647 * 0.7353(0.2647) * 0.7020$$

$$= -0.0362$$

Now for a quick calculation of **w7** and **w8**.

Calculating the gradient with respect to w7

Notice that this calculation is almost identical to **w5**. The only difference is replacing **outb1** with **outb2**.

$$\frac{\partial E}{\partial W_7} = (0.5934 - 0\,) * 0.5934(1 - 0.5934) * 0.5841$$

$$= 0.5934 * 0.5934(0.4066) * 0.5841$$

$$= 0.0836$$

Calculating the gradient with respect to w8

Notice that this calculation is almost identical to **w6**. Again, **outb1** has been replaced with **outb2**.

$$\frac{\partial E}{\partial W_8} = (0.7353 - 1) * 0.7353(1 - 0.7353) * 0.5841$$

$$= -0.2647 * 0.7353(0.247) * 0.5841$$

$$= -0.0301$$

Section 2: Calculating Gradients For Output Layer Bias Weights

This is very fast. In fact, we have already calculated it! We accomplished this when we calculated the partial derivatives for the output layer nodes.

The gradient of any output layer bias weight is simply Delta$_z$:

$$\delta_z = (z-t)\, z(1 - z)$$

Now remember, we calculated two different Delta$_z$'s: one for **node c1**, and one for **node c2**. All we need to do is connect the correct Delta$_z$ with the correct bias weight! Looking at the network layout below, we can see that **bw3** relates to Delta$_z$ for node **c1**, while **bw4** relates to Delta$_z$ for node **c2**.

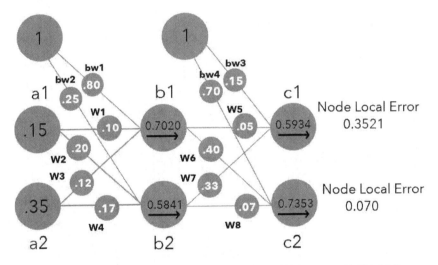

Therefore:

$$\frac{\partial E}{\partial BW_3} = \delta_z = (z-t)\, z(1 - z)$$
$$= 0.1432$$

And:

$$\frac{\partial E}{\partial BW_4} = \delta_z = (z\text{-}t)\,z(1 - z)$$

$$= -0.0515$$

Finally! We have now finished calculating the gradients (partial derivatives) for each weight connected to the output layer. Let's move forward and begin calculating the hidden layer weights.

Section 3: Calculating Gradients For Hidden Layer Weights

There are a total of four hidden layer weights situated between the input layer and hidden layer that we will be calculating gradients for. See below.

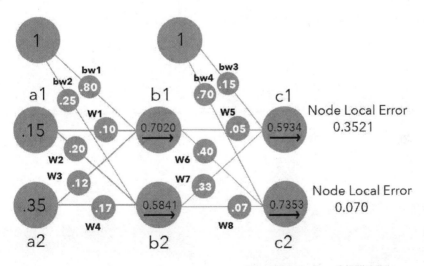

The formula we will use is as follows, with slight adjustments for **w1.** Again, we derived this formula back in Part 2: Stage 3. *Note: we have broken the formula into three parts for easy calculation.*

$$\frac{\partial E}{\partial W_1} = \underbrace{\left(\sum_c \delta_z W_i \right)}_{\textbf{1}} \underbrace{out_{b1} (1 - out_{b1})}_{\textbf{2}} \overset{\textbf{3}}{out_{a1}}$$

Calculating for W1: Part 1

Let's begin by calculating Part 1 of the formula. Note that w_i in the formula stands for an unspecified weight due to the fact we will be dealing with two weights: **w5** and **w6.** If you look at the network layout, you can see that a change in **w1** affects two output layer weights, which are **w5** and **w6.**

There are a total of two output nodes, and therefore we will need to calculate and sum the following.

$\square_z$ * **w5** for output **node c1.**

Delta$_z$ * **w6** for output **node c2.**

As we discovered when we calculated the gradient for output layer bias weights, we have already calculated Delta$_z$ for each node! A quick review:

For **node c1:**

$$\delta_z = (z\text{-}t)\, z(1 - z)$$
$$= 0.1432$$

Therefore, all we need to do is multiply by **w5:**

$$= 0.1432 * 0.05$$

$$= 0.0072$$

And for **node c2.**

$$\delta_z = (z\text{-}t)\,z(1 - z)$$

$$= -0.0515$$

We multiply our answer by **w6:**

$$= -0.0515 * 0.40$$

$$= -0.0206$$

Now we can implement the summation operator and add the two values together:

$$= 0.0072 + (\text{-}0.0206)$$

$$= -0.0134$$

Part 1 of the formula is now complete! Let's plug it into the formula.

$$\frac{\partial E}{\partial W_1} = \left(\overbrace{-0.0134}^{1} \right) \underbrace{\text{out}_{b1}\,(1 - \text{out}_{b1})}_{2}\,\overset{3}{\text{out}_{a1}}$$

Calculating for W1: Parts 2 and 3

Solving for Part 2 is quite straightforward.

The formula is:

$$\text{out}_{b1}\,(1 - \text{out}_{b1})$$

Substituting our values we get:

$$= 0.7020 * (1 - 0.7020)$$

$$= 0.2092$$

Part 2 is now calculated. If we plug it into the formula, and also plug in Part 3 (which is simply **outa1**), our formula will be finished! *Note that the final answer is very small, and thus we have extended the decimal places.*

$$\frac{\partial E}{\partial W_1} = \left(\overbrace{-0.0134}^{①} \right) \underbrace{0.2092 \qquad \overset{③}{.15}}_{②}$$

$$= -0.0134 * 0.2092 * .15$$

$$= -0.000420492$$

Calculating for W2: Part 1

Now we will move on and calculate the gradient for **w2.** The formula we will use is below. Again, we will be solving each part in order.

$$\frac{\partial E}{\partial W_2} = \left(\overbrace{\sum_c \delta_z W_i}^{①} \right) \underbrace{out_{b2}(1 - out_{b2})\overset{③}{out_{a1}}}_{②}$$

Calculating for W2: Part 1

Note that w_i in the formula stands for an unspecified weight due to the fact we will be dealing with two weights: **w7** and **w8.** If you look at the network layout, you can see that a change in **w2** affects a total of two output layer weights, which are **w7** and **w8.**

There are a total of two output nodes, and therefore we will need to calculate and sum the following.

$\square_z$ * **w7** for output **node c1**.

Delta$_z$ * **w8** for output **node c2**.

As we discovered before, we have already calculated Delta$_z$ for each node! For **node c1:**

$$\delta_z = (z-t)\, z(1 - z)$$
$$= 0.1432$$

Therefore, all we need to do is multiply by **w7**:

$$= 0.1432 * 0.33$$

$$= 0.0473$$

And for **node c2.**

$$\delta_z = (z-t)\, z(1 - z)$$
$$= -0.0515$$

We multiply our answer by **w8**:

$$= -0.0515 * 0.07$$

$$= -0.0036$$

And finally add the two values together:

= 0.0473 + (-0.0036)

= 0.0437

Part 1 of the formula is complete. If we plug it into the formula, we have the following:

$$\frac{\partial E}{\partial W_2} = \left(\overbrace{0.0437}^{\textcircled{1}} \right) \underbrace{out_{b2}(1 - out_{b2})}_{\textcircled{2}} \overset{\textcircled{3}}{out_{a1}}$$

Calculating for W2: Parts 2 and 3

Solving for Part 2 is quite straightforward.

The formula is:

$$out_{b2}(1 - out_{b2})$$

Substituting our values we get:

= 0.5841 * (1 - 0.5841)

= 0.2429

Part 2 is calculated! Our formula now looks as follows (including part 3, which is simply **out_{a1}**). *Note that the final answer is very small, and thus we have extended the decimal places.*

$$\frac{\partial E}{\partial W_2} = \left(\overset{\textbf{①}}{0.0437} \right) \underset{\textbf{②}}{0.2429} \quad \overset{\textbf{③}}{.15}$$

$$= 0.0437 * 0.2429 * .15$$

$$= 0.00159221$$

Our gradients for **w1** and **w2** are calculated. Now we will quickly calculate the remaining gradients for weights **w3 and w4.**

Calculating for w3

Notice that this calculation is almost identical to **w1.** The only difference is replacing **outa1** with **outa2.**

$$\frac{\partial E}{\partial W_3} = -0.0134 * 0.2092 * 0.35$$
$$= -0.000981148$$

Calculating for w4

Notice that this calculation is almost identical to **w2.** The only difference is replacing **outa1** with **outa2.**

$$\frac{\partial E}{\partial W_4} = 0.0437 * 0.2429 * 0.35$$
$$= 0.003715156$$

Section 4: Calculating Gradients For Hidden Layer Bias Weights

Akin to output layer bias weights, this will be fast! The gradient of any hidden layer bias weight is simply the Delta$_b$ of the previous layer:

$$\delta_b = \left(\sum_c \delta_z W_i \right) out_i (1 - out_i)$$

1 All of the letter **"i"'s** refer to a unique value. This value depends on the gradient we are calculating.

Now remember, we calculated two different Delta_b's for the previous layer: one for **node b1** and one for **node b2**. All we need to do is connect the correct Delta_b with the correct bias weight! This is what the *unique value* is referring to in the formula above. Looking at the network layout below, we can see that **bw1** relates to Delta_b for node **b1**, while **bw2** relates to Delta_b for node **b2**.

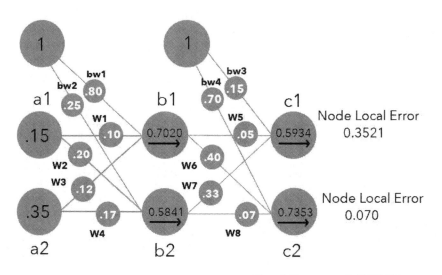

Therefore:

$$\frac{\partial E}{\partial BW_1} = \left(\sum_c \delta_z W_{5+6} \right) out_{b1} (1 - out_{b1})$$

$$= (-0.0134) * 0.7020 (1 - 0.7020)$$

$$= -0.0028$$

You can see above that we have included the actual weights (5 + 6) used to calculate Delta_b for **node b1** output. This is simply for clarity.

And:

$$\frac{\partial E}{\partial BW_2} = \left(\sum_C \delta_z W_{7+8}\right) out_{b2}(1 - out_{b2})$$

$$= 0.0437 * 0.5841\,(1\text{-}0.5841)$$
$$= 0.0106$$

Again, we have included the actual weights (7 + 8) used to calculate Delta_b for **node b2** output.

Section 5: All Gradients

Calculating the gradients is now complete! Here are all of the gradients we have calculated:

Total Gradients Calculated	
$\dfrac{\partial E}{\partial W_1}$ - 0.000420492	$\dfrac{\partial E}{\partial W_2}$ = 0.00159221
$\dfrac{\partial E}{\partial W_3}$ = - 0.000981148	$\dfrac{\partial E}{\partial W_4}$ = 0.003715156
$\dfrac{\partial E}{\partial W_5}$ = 0.1005	$\dfrac{\partial E}{\partial W_6}$ = - 0.0362
$\dfrac{\partial E}{\partial W_7}$ = 0.0836	$\dfrac{\partial E}{\partial W_8}$ = - 0.0301
$\dfrac{\partial E}{\partial BW_1}$ = - 0.0028	$\dfrac{\partial E}{\partial BW_2}$ = 0.016
$\dfrac{\partial E}{\partial BW_3}$ = 0.1432	$\dfrac{\partial E}{\partial BW_4}$ = - 0.0515

Stage 4: Gradient Checking

After calculating gradients, our next step is to check the gradients. We learned about this in Ch 8. Stage 4: Checking Gradients. Since this step is optional, we will only complete the process for a single weight from our network.

Specifications:
- We will use weight 5 and label it as **w5**.
- We will use 10^{-4} for the Epsilon value.

The general formula for gradient checking is as follows. Note that we have divided it into two parts for easy calculations.

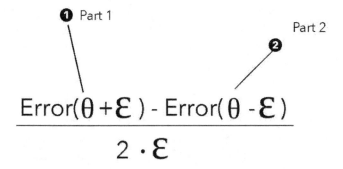

To compute this we will begin with Part 1 and follow the same 7 steps we outlined in Stage 4.

Part 1:

Step 1. Add Epsilon

To start, we add the Epsilon value to the weight we are checking the gradient for.

$$W5_{new} = W5 + \varepsilon$$
$$= 0.05 + 0.0001$$
$$= 0.0501$$

Step 2. Recalculate the Total Error of the network

Next, we recalculate the total error of the network using the new **w5** value we calculated in Step 1. This means we would work again through Stages 1-2. Note that we did not round any of the new calculations.

This is somewhat challenging to show, but the final result is:

$$\text{Error}(\theta + \varepsilon) = \text{Error}(W1, W2, W3, W4, W5 + \varepsilon)$$
$$= 0.211045192$$

We now have the following part of our formula:

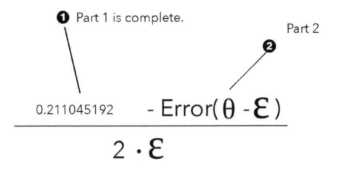

1 Part 1 is complete.

Part 2

2

$$\frac{0.211045192 \quad - \text{Error}(\theta - \varepsilon)}{2 \cdot \varepsilon}$$

Part 2

Step 3. Subtract Epsilon

Moving forward, we recalculate the total error again but this time we subtract the Epsilon value from the weight we are concerned with.

$$W5_{new} = W5 - \varepsilon$$
$$= 0.05 - 0.0001$$
$$= 0.0499$$

Step 4. Recalculate the Total Error of the network

Finally, we recalculate the total error of the network by using the value we calculated in Step 3. This means we would work again through Stages 1-2.

The final value we arrive at it:

$$\text{Error}(\theta - \mathcal{E}) = \text{Error}(W1, W2, W3, W4, W5 - \mathcal{E})$$
$$= 0.211025091$$

We have now completed the formula:

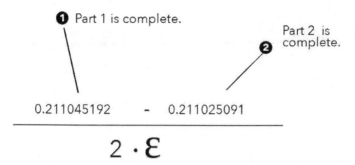

Part 1 is complete.

Part 2 is complete.

$$\frac{0.211045192 \quad - \quad 0.211025091}{2 \cdot \mathcal{E}}$$

Step 5: Calculate the Numerical Approximation

Now that we have our entire formula, we can calculate the numerical approximation for the weight we are concerned with. To do this, the formula that we have completed is worked out.

$$= \frac{0.211045192 \quad - \quad 0.211025091}{2 \cdot \mathcal{E}}$$

$$= \frac{0.211045192 \quad - \quad 0.211025091}{2 * 0.0001}$$

$$= \frac{0.000020101}{0.0002}$$

$$= 0.100505$$

Step 6: Measure Against the Analytic Gradient

Next, we check the numerical approximation against the analytical gradient. Doing this will tell us how "far off" the two gradients are from each other. If you recall, the analytical gradient is the original gradient that the network computed.

Difference = Analytical Gradient - Numerical Gradient

= 0.1005 - 0.100505

= -0.000005

Then, we convert the value to scientific notation. Note that we are only considering the magnitude of the number, not the fact that it is negative:

Conversion = 5×10^{-6}

Step 7: Compute The Relative Error

The output from Step 6 is 10^{-6}, which is *very small* and difficult to interpret. Is it good? Bad? Ok? To help bring clarity, we will calculate the Relative Error. The Relative Error is calculated by dividing the difference by whichever is larger.

$$= \frac{\text{Analytical Gradient - Numerical Gradient}}{\text{max(Analytical Gradient, Numerical Gradient)}}$$

$$= \frac{0.211045192 - 0.211025091}{0.211045192}$$

$$= \frac{0.000020101}{0.211045192}$$

= 0.000095245

Then, we convert to scientific notation and compare the result to our relative error table:

Conversion = 9.5×10^{-5}

When we look at our table of relative errors, we see the following:

Relative Error	Rules of Thumb
$> 10^{-2}$	High chance the gradient is wrong.
$< 10^{-2}$ and $> 10^{-4}$	A double red flag. Something is wrong.
Between 10^{-5} and 10^{-6}	A single red flag. Use caution.
$< = 10^{-7}$	High chance the gradient is correct.

Therefore, a relative error on the order of 10^{-5} is not bad, although not great, and we should be cautious moving forward.

Stage 5: Updating Weights

It is now time to update the weights! This is the final step in backpropagation, and the last stage in our network. To accomplish this we are going to make use of the general update formula that we covered in Section 2: Stage 5.

This stage is divided into the following sections:
1. Updating General Weights
2. Updating Bias Weights

Updating General Weights

The formula is provided below. We will begin with updating weight **w8,** which you can see within the formula itself. *Note that the update formula does not include momentum. We have omitted this for sake of ease and calculation.*

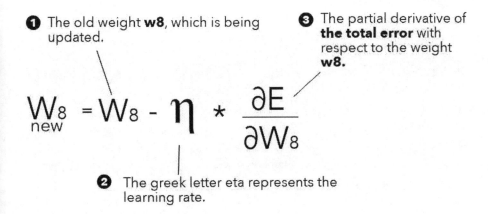

❶ The old weight **w8**, which is being updated.

❸ The partial derivative of **the total error** with respect to the weight **w8.**

$$W_{8\,new} = W_8 - \eta * \frac{\partial E}{\partial W_8}$$

❷ The greek letter eta represents the learning rate.

Let's start!

Updating Weight W8

To update weight **w8,** we will substitute our values into the formula above:

$$W8_{new} = 0.07 - 0.5 * (-0.0301)$$

$$= 0.07 - (-0.01505)$$

$$= 0.0851$$

And that is all there is too it! The new value for **w8** has increased by 0.0126 to 0.0826.

Let's finish this off by calculating the remaining new weights.

Updating Weight W7

$$W7_{new} = 0.33 - 0.5 * 0.0836$$

$$= 0.33 - 0.0418$$

$$= 0.2882$$

Updating Weight W6

$$W6_{new} = 0.40 - 0.5 * (-0.0362)$$

$$= 0.40 - (-0.0181)$$

$$= 0.4181$$

Updating Weight W5

$$W5_{new} = 0.05 - 0.5 * 0.1005$$

$$= 0.05 - 0.05025$$

$$= -0.00025$$

Updating Weight W4

W_4 new $= 0.17 - 0.5 * 0.003715156$

$\quad\quad = 0.17 - 0.01857578$

$\quad\quad = 0.1514$

Updating Weight W_3

W_3 new $= 0.12 - 0.5 * (-0.000981148)$

$\quad\quad = 0.12 - (-0.000490574)$

$\quad\quad = 0.1205$

Updating Weight W_2

W_2 new $= 0.20 - 0.5 * (0.00159221)$

$\quad\quad = 0.20 - (0.000796105)$

$\quad\quad = 0.1992$

Updating Weight W_1

W_1 new $= 0.10 - 0.5 * (-0.0000420492)$

$\quad\quad = 0.10 - (- 0.000210246)$

$\quad\quad = 0.1002$

Updating Bias Weights

To update the bias weights we apply the exact same formula as above. Let's begin.

*Updating Weight **BW4***

$$BW4_{new} = 0.70 - 0.5 * (- 0.0515)$$
$$= 0.70 - (-0.02575)$$
$$= 0.7258$$

*Updating Weight **BW3***

$$BW3_{new} = 0.15 - 0.5 * 0.1432$$
$$= 0.15 - 0.0716$$
$$= 0.0784$$

*Updating Weight **BW2***

$$BW2_{new} = 0.25 - 0.5 * 0.016$$
$$= 0.25 - 0.008$$
$$= 0.242$$

*Updating Weight **BW1***

$$BW1_{new} = 0.80 - 0.5 * (- 0.0028)$$
$$= 0.80 - (-0.014)$$
$$= 0.814$$

Wrapping it All up: Final Review

Let's recap what we have accomplished in Part 3.

First, we created a fictitious purpose for our network: classifying two types of images. This (hopefully!) provided a tangible context that we could build our network upon. We then built our network structure, but immediately scaled it down so that it could be effectively used as a training example. Our scaled network included two input nodes, two hidden nodes, and two output nodes.

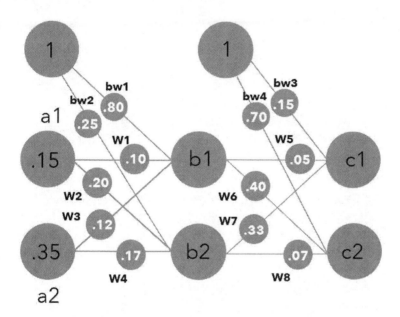

After this we began to pass our chicken image through the network, with the goal of an output of [0, 1].

We used the summation operator and Logistic activation function to pass our information through the network.

$$\sum$$

$$f(x) = \frac{1}{1 + e^{-x}}$$

However, the network output was not [0, 1], but the following:

$$\begin{bmatrix} 0.5934 \\ 0.7353 \end{bmatrix}$$

Next, we calculated the total network error using the SE cost function.

$$SE = \frac{1}{2} \sum_{i=1}^{n} (t_i - z_i)^2$$

Following this, we began the update process by calculating the error for each weight (which is technically called the gradient, and arrived at by calculating the partial derivative).

We calculated the gradients, and then checked to see if the gradients were accurate using the following formulas.

Gradient Calculation *hidden layer weights.*

$$\frac{\partial E}{\partial W_1} = \left(\sum_c \delta_z W_5\right) \text{out}_{b1} (1 - \text{out}_{b1}) \text{out}_{a1}$$

Gradient Checking Formula

$$\frac{\text{Error}(\theta + \varepsilon) - \text{Error}(\theta - \varepsilon)}{2 \cdot \varepsilon}$$

Finally, we arrived at the point of updating the weights. To do this we used the following formula:

$$W_{new} = W_{old} - \eta * \frac{\partial E}{\partial W_{old}}$$

Once we updated the weights, our example concluded. However, in real life the network would continue to loop through Stages 2 - 5 until the network converges when the error rate reaches an acceptable level.

Part 3
Building Neural Networks

Building A Neural Network: The Tools You'll Need

There are many ways to build a neural network and lots of tools to get the job done. This is fantastic, but it can also be overwhelming when you start, because there are *so many* tools to choose from. In this chapter, we are going to take a look at what tools are needed and help you nail down the essentials.

To build a neural network, you need *at least* the following:
1. A programming language
2. A text editor
3. A dataset

Optional tools include:
1. A machine learning library
2. A mathematical library

Let's take a brief look at each of these tools.

Programming Language
We recommend Python.

Stating this might be too obvious, but neural networks are simply computer code. To create a network (or any other type of machine learning algorithm for that matter), you'll need to choose a language you will use. Python is by far the most popular, but there are many other languages to choose from such as:

-   R (also popular)
-   Scala
-   C++
-   C
-   Java

Text Editor
We recommend Jupyter.

Text editors are like a baseball mit; there are many to choose from, and you want to select one that fits well and works for your needs. Some are packed with features, while others are bare-bones, and it's up to you to make a decision.

A text editor is where you write your code, and it is different from a word processor or IDE.

- **Text Editor:** A text editor is a lightweight application that offers one of the easiest ways to write code. With text editors, formatting is stripped down to the basics, and coding is typically fast and simple. Many text editors offer code-completion, text-coloring, package managers, and work on multiple platforms (Mac, Linux, Windows).
    - Popular editors include:
        - Jupyter
        - Sublime

- **IDE:** IDE stands for Integrated Development Environment. In short, they are more robust than text editors and contain many more powerful features than text editors do. IDEs allow you to write code, then run it and debug it all within the same environment. IDEs often contain the following:
    - A text editor
    - A compiler
    - A debugger
    - A GUI

  IDEs are developed for specific languages, and popular Python environments include PyCharm, PyDev, and Spyder Python.

- **Word Processor:** In contrast, word processors are writing applications, such as Microsoft Word, OpenOffice, and Google Docs. These applications are not designed for coding. They do not work well due to formatted text (bold, italics, underline, etc.).

Dataset
We will be using the MNIST dataset.

Neural networks need lots of data to work with, but where do you find datasets that are free and large enough? For our example, we will be using the free MNIST handwriting set, but if you are looking for other options for text, images, sound, etc., here are a few popular websites:

-University of Southern California, Irvine (UCLI) Database
- Pew Research Datasets
- Healthdata.gov
- Public Amazon Datasets
- Kaggle

Libraries
We recommend Tensorflow.

A library is like a toolkit. There are many different libraries, and each library has a different set of tools and purpose. When coding, you can call (import) a library and make use of the tools it has to offer.

More technically speaking, a library is a set of previously written code that can be called upon and used by programmers. It is a collection of object files and can consist of functions, variables, classes, or operations—the "tools" others have written that you can use. A fabulous example is Numpy, which is the go-to resource for math and scientific computing. Programmers can use Numpy to perform many tasks, such as rounding, creating arrays, and even permutations.

Other non-technical definitions of a library include:
- A library is a file that contains popular and useful code.
- A library is a shortcut for implementing popular functions.
- A library is a set of reusable code for popular tasks.

Mathematical Library
Math on a large scale can be incredibly challenging to calculate and keep error-free. There are a number of mathematical libraries that can be used to reduce errors and speed up calculations. Some of the most popular include:

- Numpy
- Scipy
- PyBrain (no longer developed but still useful)

Machine Learning Library

Machine learning is a complex undertaking, but thankfully there are many top-notch libraries developed specifically for ML that make the process much easier and faster. We use and recommend Tensorflow, but there are many more popular libraries including:

- Theano
- Caffe
- Torch
- Keras
- SciKit Learn

Wrap-Up

To wrap this section up, there are three tools that we recommend:

Tool #1: Python
Tool #2: Jupyter
Tool #3: Tensorflow

Tensorflow: A Very Brief Overview

Tensorflow is an open source library developed by Google that excels at numerical computation. On a high level, it is a tool that can perform complex mathematical computations really quickly and efficiently.

It can be run on all kinds of computers, including smartphones, and is quickly becoming a popular tool within machine learning. Tensorflow supports deep learning (neural nets with multiple hidden layers) as well as reinforcement learning, and is used in Google's speech recognition systems, Google Photos, Gmail, Google search, and more.

The Basics: How Tensorflow Works

Tensorflow is a machine learning library that can be used for all sorts of machine learning tasks, but is primarily designed for creating deep neural networks. At its core, Tensorflow is built on three key components:

- A computational graph
- Nodes
- Edges

Computational Graph

A computational graph defines all of the mathematical computations that will happen. It does not perform the computations and it doesn't hold any values - it simply defines what operations will take place. A computational graph contains nodes and edges.

Nodes

The Nodes of a computational graph represent mathematical operations. Many of these operations are complex and happen over and over again. This is where Tensorflow is so incredible; it removes much of the complexity and makes it easy to repeat the operations efficiently. In Tensorflow, these nodes are called ops (short for operations).

Edges

Edges represent tensors, which hold the data (information) that is sent between the nodes. We'll dive into tensors more when we explore the math of neural networks, but on a high-level, they are multidimensional arrays of numbers that represent information.

How This All Works Together

1. A computational graph is built.
2. The graph contains nodes, which are mathematical operations.
3. The graph contains edges, which hold information in the form of tensors.
4. When the graph is run, each node receives some tensor(s), performs some operation(s), and spits out some new tensor(s). The new tensor(s) are in turn received by different node(s), and the cycle continues. (Note that not all nodes have to receive a tensor, nor do they have to spit out a new tensor, but that is beyond the scope of this brief overview.)

How A Neural Network is Built in Tensorflow

With Tensorflow, a neural network is built by creating a computational graph, and the graph contains nodes and edges. Once complete, you run the graph, which in our case means running a neural network.

Computational Graph
Image source: tensorflow.org

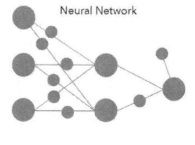

Neural Network

With Tensorflow, a neural network is built by creating a computational graph

In the context of a neural network, the nodes on a computation graph represent all of the mathematical operations that occur within the network. These can include matrix multiplication, bias addition, and activation functions (all of which you can learn more of in earlier chapters).

In the context of a neural network, the edges on a computation graph represent all of the data that flows through the network. This data starts its journey as input data into the first layer and then moves through the network.

How To Install Tensorflow

There are multiple ways to install Tensorflow. Are you on a PC? Mac? Running Ubuntu? Running Docker?

Rather than try to explain each method, the best way is to simply point you to tensorflow.org/install. You'll find fantastic step-by-step instructions for every possible setup.

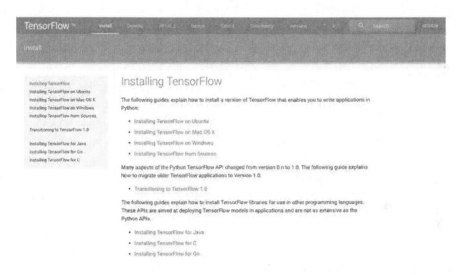

*image taken from tensorflow.org/install

**This introduction is VERY brief. If you want to know more, O'Reilly has a fantastic introduction that is very easy to understand. The official Tensorflow website is also helpful, as is this tutorial series from learningtensorflow.com.

Ch. 27

Tensorflow + Neural Networks: 5 Steps

There is no single way to build a feedforward neural network with Python, and that is especially true if you throw Tensorflow into the mix. However, there is a general framework that exists that can be divided into five steps and grouped into two parts. In this chapter, we are going to briefly explore these five steps so that we are prepared to use them to build a network later on.

Ready ? Let's begin.

Part 1: Building the Tensorflow Graph
  Step 1: Import Dependencies
  Step 2: Define Hyperparameters and Placeholders
  Step 3: Create a Network Model
  Step 4: Define Training Elements

Part 2: Launching the Tensorflow Graph
  Step 5: Create a Session and Train

Part 1: Building The Tensorflow Graph
If you haven't installed Tensorflow yet, visit tensorflow.org/install for instructions.

Step 1: Import Dependencies
Importing dependencies is always the first step when creating a network, with or without Tensorflow. On a high level, dependencies are essentially libraries of code that other people have written which you import into your project. In Python, they come in the form of modules or functions. Below is an example of importing the Tensorflow module and referring to it as **tf**:

```
import tensorflow as tf
```

Step 2: Define Hyperparameters and Placeholders

After importing dependencies, the next step is to define network hyperparameters and placeholders. Hyperparameters are the network "settings" which are given rather than learned, and placeholders are where data is fed through (more later). From Step 1, Tensorflow automatically generates a default *computational graph*, and here in Step 2 we begin to modify this graph.

A computational graph is a graph that defines computations and nothing more; it doesn't actually compute anything, nor does it hold any values. It simply defines computations that will be run when the graph is launched via a session in Step 5.

Hyperparameters are predefined and do not change as the network is trained. These can include the following:
- General parameters, such as learning rate, batch size, and number of training iterations.
- Network parameters, such as the number of layers and nodes.

Placeholders are empty tensors that will be fed data as the network operates, and they are created with Tensorflow's placeholder operation. Typical placeholders include the network input and target output. Below is an example of defining the network input **"X"** with the placeholder operation.

```
X = tf.placeholder(tf.float32, shape=(64, 784))
```

Step 3: Create the Network Model

The next step is to create the network model. This includes two parts: *parameters* that the network will adjust as it trains, and the *feedforward calculations* of the network. Parameters that the network will adjust as it trains include the weights and biases, which are basically how important each piece of information is to the calculations.

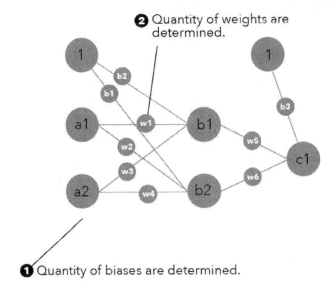

2 Quantity of weights are determined.

1 Quantity of biases are determined.

However, at this point only the number of weights and biases is determined, along with how they will be calculated. Their actual values will be generated when the network begins to learning by training. This will be explained in more depth when we build out first network in Chapter 2.

The feedforward calculations define how values will move through the network, and typically include matrix multiplication and activation functions.

A variety of Tensorflow operations are used to complete both parts of the model, such as *tf.random_normal* and *tf.zero*. Tensorflow's Variable class is also commonly used. Below is an example of computing a layer's output using the **tf.matmul** operation.

```
output2 = tf.nn.sigmoid(tf.matmul(output1, weights2) +
biases1)
```

Step 4: Define Training Elements
In the fourth step, various elements are defined that are necessary to train the network, including the network's prediction, cost function, optimization function, and training step size. A variety of Tensorflow operations are used to do this, such as *tf.train* and *tf.reduce_mean*. Below is an example of defining the optimizer using the **gradient descent** optimizer subclass.

```
optimizer =
tf.train.GradientDescentOptimizer(0.0001).minimize(cost)
```

Part 2: Running the Tensorflow Graph

Step 5: Create a Session and Train

The last step is to create a Tensorflow "session" object that runs the computational graph we have created in Steps 2-4. A session allows us to execute the computations we have defined in the graph.

In a session, the following typically occurs: Tensorflow variables are initialized, batches of training data are created to loop over, and training is begun by feeding placeholders with data.

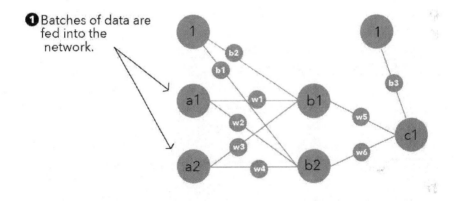

Below is an example of all variables being initialized using the **tf.global_variables_initializer** function.

```
sess.run(tf.global_variables_initializer())
```

Ch. 28

Building a Neural Network with Tensorflow: Distinguish Handwriting

In this chapter, we are going to dig deep with Tensorflow and build a neural network that can distinguish between handwritten numbers. We'll use the same 5 steps we covered in the high-level overview, and we are going to take time exploring each line of code.

This is a tutorial on the MNIST dataset that is designed for beginners. In this tutorial we explain the basics, line by line, and do not gloss over definitions or assume you understand every line of code.

You will find the final code for this on Github at https://github.com/mh-taylor/MNIST_Code_Final/tree/master.

We break everything apart so that you can confidently make changes and tweaks when you begin experimenting on your own. After all, it's easy to copy and paste a line of code from Github, but if you don't know what it does exactly, how can you troubleshoot or tweak it later on?

So, let's get started!

Part 1: Building the Tensorflow Graph

Step 1: Import Dependencies
To start, we will import our dependencies. Remember, dependencies are code others have written that we are going to import and use in our project. Importing dependencies saves us countless hours of writing code (not to mention potential errors).

We will also be importing the image data for our network. When we are finished, the code for Part 1 will appear as follows:

```
1. import tensorflow as tf
2. from tensorflow.examples.tutorials.mnist import
input_data
3. mnist = input_data.read_data_sets("/tmp/data/",
one_hot=True)
```

Line 1

We'll start by examining line 1.

```
1. import tensorflow as tf
```

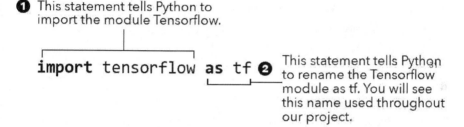

❶ This statement tells Python to import the module Tensorflow.

import tensorflow as tf ❷

❷ This statement tells Python to rename the Tensorflow module as tf. You will see this name used throughout our project.

What is Line 1 Accomplishing?

Line 1 uses Python's **import** statement to import the **tensorflow** module into our project. Tensorflow is going to help us handle all of the complex mathematical calculations needed for our network, such as matrix multiplication and activation functions. By importing Tensorflow, we will have access to the complex mathematical functions we need.

The above is quite straightforward and does not require any further unpacking. However, we should note that renaming **tensorflow** as **tf** is not necessary; in fact, **tf** could be anything! However, **tf** is commonplace, faster to type, and intuitive.

Line 2

```
2. from tensorflow.examples.tutorials.mnist import
input_data
```

❶ This statement is a path that leads to where the module **input_data** is found.

```
from tensorflow.examples.tutorials.mnist import input_data
```

❷ This statement tells Python to import a single module, **input_data**, from the path it just accessed.

What is Line 2 Accomplishing ?

Line 2 uses Python's **from** and **import** statements to import all the data we need for our network. Specifically, it imports a module called **input_data**. This module is essentially a list of other **import** statements that are all focused on successfully downloading and reading MNIST data! If you are curious about the **input_data** module you can view it on github.

Our dataset contains 70,00 images in total: 55,000 are training images, 10,000 are testing images, and 5,000 are for validation.

Samples from the MNIST dataset:

Remember: Each of the 55,000 training images and 10,000 testing images in the dataset have a target label. This target label is the "correct" output that the network will aim for when presented with its corresponding input. For example, if the number "9" is fed through the network, the network output will be compared with the "9's" target label (9), and any differences will be calculated as a *cost*, or *loss*.

Line 3

```
3. mnist = input_data.read_data_sets("/tmp/data/",
one_hot=True)
```

❶ This statement tells Python to use a function named
read_data_sets from the **input_data** module we just
imported.

mnist = input_data.read_data_sets("/tmp/data/", one_hot=True)

❷ These are two arguments for the
read_data_sets function.
Both are explained below.

What is Line 3 Accomplishing ?
Line 3 creates a DataSet as a variable named **mnist** that stores the data
we imported on Line 2. As with the name **tf**, **mnist** is commonplace and
used by Tensorflow.org (plus it's intuitive, so we will use it too).

What is "input_data.read_data_sets" ?
Read_data_sets is a function within the module **input_data**, and it
reads the dataset imported on line 2. On a high level, it prepares and
modifies the input data so that we can make use of it! To do this it
performs a variety of actions such as defining what constitutes the testing,
training, and validation sets.

The function **read_data_sets** has a single required argument and five
optional arguments with default values.

Required: directory location. In our case, this is **/tmp/data/.**
Defaults values:
- fake_data=False
- one_hot=False
- dtype=float32
- reshape=True
- validaiton_size=5000

Let's pause and explore both arguments used in our code.

What is "tmp/data/" ?

The first argument, **"/tmp/data/",** is the directory on your computer where Tensorflow will read the data set as it works with and trains the network. For this example, we have made this directory inside our temporary folder. Always make sure you have permission to create a new directory!

What is "one_hot=True" ?

The second argument, **"one_hot=True",** turns on one-hot encoding. On a high level, one-hot encoding transforms the target output labels of a network into a vector with values of 1 and 0. A single "hot" output node with a value of 1 represents the network's target output, while the rest of the output nodes are 0s (zeros). One-hot encoding works very well for classification problems, and is widely used in machine learning.

For example, if a net classifies apples and oranges, and an orange is the input, the right one-hot output is 01; whereas, if an apple is the input, the right one-hot output is 10. For recognizing digits, our one-hot encoding is as follows:

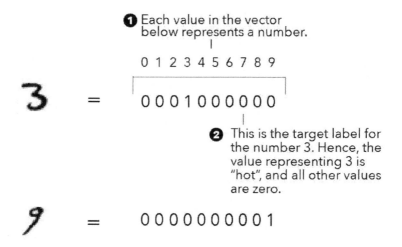

Part 1 is complete. We now have all the tools we need to perform the complex math calculations in our network, plus we have our dataset with our one-hot target labels! Our code now looks as follows:

```
1. import tensorflow as tf
2. from tensorflow.examples.tutorials.mnist import
input_data
3. mnist = input_data.read_data_sets("/tmp/data/",
one_hot=True)
```

Step 2: Define Hyperparameters and Placeholders

The next step is to define our hyperparameters and placeholders, and we will start with the former. We will only provide a brief explanation of each parameter, but if you would like to learn more, please visit our math chapter and/or extended definitions section.

General Parameters

Our general parameters include the following.
- **Learning rate.** On a high level, this tells the network how large of a *step* it should take towards its target when adjusting the layer weights. The goal is to minimize the error between the correct output and the actual output of the network. The closer this error is to 0 (zero), the better, but if the learning rate is too high, it will overshoot and miss this minimum; too low and it will slowly get stuck in a local minimum that may not be as good
- **Batch size.** This tells the network how many training images to use at once to update the weights of a network. For example, if the batch size is 100, the network will update its weights every 100 images, i.e. every time it completes a batch. Updating in batches instead of the whole huge data set saves memory (but requires more iterations).
- **Update step.** This tells the network how often to print an update of its training progress. For example, an update value of 5 will print an update every 5 epochs. An epoch occurs when an entire training set has gone forward and backward through a network. Remember, our training set is 55,000 images.

Note: Many of these parameters do not need to be defined because their values can simply be "plugged" into the code. However, we have chosen to include them for simplicity and clarity but will always point out where they could be plugged straight in.

Let's see what the above looks like as code:

```
5. learning_rate = 0.0001
6. batch_size = 100
7. update_step = 10
```

Each of the above is straightforward, so we won't bother drilling down any further.

Next, we will define our network parameters.

Network Parameters
Our network parameters include the following:

-   **Number of hidden layers.**
-   **Number of nodes per hidden layer**
-   **Number of output nodes.**

The selection of layers and nodes is a complex and difficult subject (you can read more in our math section). For the sake of ease, we will be creating a network with three hidden layers and 500 nodes per layer, while our output layer will consist of 10 nodes. Why 10 ? This is because we are classifying 10 numbers (0-9), and each number is a "class" that is represented by an output node.

Here is what our network parameters look like in code:

```
9.  layer_1_nodes = 500
10. layer_2_nodes = 500
11. layer_3_nodes = 500
12. output_nodes = 10
```

Since each line above is straightforward and does not require any further explanation, we will keep moving forward.

Placeholders

Placeholders are empty tensors that will be fed data as the network operates, and they are created with Tensorflow's placeholder operation. Placeholder's require a single argument and have two optional arguments with default values:

Required: Data type (dtype)
Default Values:
- shape = None
- name = None

A general feedforward neural network requires only two placeholders: one for the network's input layer, and one for the network's target output layer. This looks as follows:

```
14. network_input = tf.placeholder(tf.float32, [None, 784])
15. target_output = tf.placeholder(tf.float32, [None,
output_nodes])
```

Line 14
Let's take a closer look at Line 14:

❶ This statement tells Python to use a method named **placeholder** from the Tensorflow module we renamed as **tf**. Tensorflow calls these methods an **operation,** and we will too moving forward.

```
network_input = tf.placeholder(tf.float32, [None, 784])
```

❷ These are two arguments for the **placeholder** operation.
The first, **tf.float32** is the datatype.
The second in **square brackets** [] is the shape of the tensor. Read more on this below.

What is Line 14 accomplishing ?
Line 14 uses a placeholder operation to define the shape and data type of the network's input layer. The first operation argument, **"tf.float32"**, defines the datatype of the tensor, and uses a second **tf** operation to do so.

The second argument, **"[None, 784]"**, defines the shape of the input layer, which is a tensor. Let's dig deeper into both.

What is "tf.float32" ?
Tf.float32 defines the datatype of a tensor, and **"float32"** refers to a 32-bit floating point number. Floating point is a technique that allows the decimal point of a number to essentially *float, or move.* On a high level, floating point helps computers work with and represent numbers that contain fractions.

There are many advantages to using a floating point datatype, but we will not dive into those here.

The number **"32"** refers to the type of floating point used. Tensorflow offers two options: 32 bit and 64 bit. Each varies in the amount of precision it stores and has its own pros and cons, such as resolution and storage capabilities. For this tutorial we have selected **float32**.

What is [None, 784] ?
"None" and **"784"** define the shape (length and width) of the **network_input**, which is a 2-dimensional tensor. The first dimension is the length and represents the total number of images in a batch, which is currently not known but will be defined later, so it is "**None**." **"784"** is the width of the input, which is calculated by multiplying the width by length of an input image (28 x 28 = 784).

As you can see in the illustration below, **784** is derived from the total number of pixels of a 28x28 image. The individual pixels are outlined, and if you are reading on a colored device, they are red.

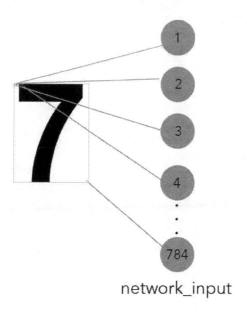

network_input

*Note: "784" could have been defined as a parameter in Step 2, much like we defined output nodes with **output_nodes.** However, we want to show how defining certain parameters is optional.*

Summing Up Line 14:
Line 14 defines **network_input,** which is a tensor. This tensor is defined with a height of 784 but a length to be determined, and a data type of 32-bit float. It is a stored in an empty placeholder that will be fed data once the network begins to train.

Line 15
This will be short!

```
15. target_output = tf.placeholder(tf.float32, [None,
output_nodes])
```

As you can see, **target_output** is almost identical to **network_input** from Line 14. The only difference is the width, which is defined using **output_nodes. Output_nodes** is a hyperparameter that we already defined in this step. That's all!

Our code now looks as follows:

```
1.  import tensorflow as tf
2.  from tensorflow.examples.tutorials.mnist import
input_data
3.  mnist = input_data.read_data_sets("/tmp/data/",
one_hot=True)
4.
5.  learning_rate = 0.0001
6.  batch_size = 100
7.  update_step = 10
8.
9.  layer_1_nodes = 500
10. layer_2_nodes = 500
11. layer_3_nodes = 500
12. output_nodes = 10
13.
14. network_input = tf.placeholder(tf.float32, [None, 784])
15. target_output = tf.placeholder(tf.float32, [None,
output_nodes])
```

Step 3: Create the Network Model

The network model can be divided into two parts: parameters that the network will adjust as it trains and feedforward calculations. We'll tackle the parameters first.

Network Parameters

Before we begin, it is worthwhile to note the following:
- We have already created the (empty) structure of the input layer. See Line 14.
- We have already defined the number of hidden layers and their number of nodes, as well as output nodes. See Lines 9-12.
Now, we must define the parameters that the network will tweak as it trains. These parameters are the weights and biases for the hidden layers and output layer. This includes both the quantity of weights and biases, as well as their values.

Here is what we will be doing in code:

Note: out_layer is output_layer, but we have shortened it so that it fits on a single line.

```
17. layer_1 = tf.Variable(tf.random_normal([784,
layer_1_nodes]))
18. layer_1_bias =
tf.Variable(tf.random_normal([layer_1_nodes]))
19. layer_2 = tf.Variable(tf.random_normal([layer_1_nodes,
layer_2_nodes]))
20. layer_2_bias =
tf.Variable(tf.random_normal([layer_2_nodes]))
21. layer_3 = tf.Variable(tf.random_normal([layer_2_nodes,
layer_3_nodes]))
22. layer_3_bias =
tf.Variable(tf.random_normal([layer_3_nodes]))
23. out_layer = tf.Variable(tf.random_normal([layer_3_nodes,
output_nodes]))
24. out_layer_bias =
tf.Variable(tf.random_normal([output_nodes]))
```

You can see that the lines of code are very similar. In light of this, we will take a look at lines 17 and 18, which will give you a good idea of how the remaining lines work.

Line 17

```
17. layer_1 = tf.Variable(tf.random_normal([784,
layer_1_nodes]))
```

Let's take a closer look on the next page

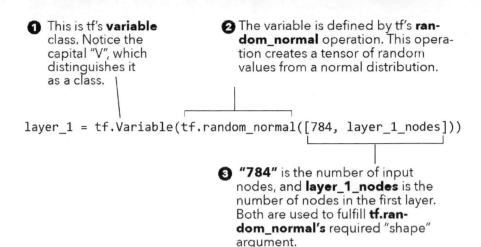

① This is tf's **variable** class. Notice the capital "V", which distinguishes it as a class.

② The variable is defined by tf's **random_normal** operation. This operation creates a tensor of random values from a normal distribution.

```
layer_1 = tf.Variable(tf.random_normal([784, layer_1_nodes]))
```

③ "784" is the number of input nodes, and **layer_1_nodes** is the number of nodes in the first layer. Both are used to fulfill **tf.random_normal's** required "shape" argument.

What is Line 17 accomplishing ?

Line 17 defines the number of adjustable parameters between the **network_input** and hidden **layer_1**. These parameters are the weights that sit on every edge, or connection, between each node in **network_input** and node in hidden **layer_1.** Line 17 also defines how the initial values of each parameter will be generated.

As you can see in the code for Line 17, **layer_1** is defined by the **tf.Variable** class, which itself is defined by the **tf.random_normal** operation, which *itself* is defined by a single argument. Let's take a few moments to assess each of these parts.

What is "tf.Variable" ?

Tf.Variable is a Tensorflow class that creates a new tensor that holds and updates parameters. In our case, the parameters are the "weights" of the network that sit on the connecting edge between every input node and first hidden layer node. **Tf.Variable** requires a single argument called *initial value,* and also has a wide-variety of optional arguments with default values. To explore this more visit tensorflow.org.

The *initial value* defines both the data type and shape of the variable tensor. However, if a shape is also specified, the initial value only defines the data type.

In our case, the initial value defines both the data type and shape of the tensor, and the values are sampled from a **tf.random_normal** distribution.

What is "tf.random_normal" ?

Tf.random_normal is one of many Tensorflow operations that can create a random distribution of numbers. This random distribution is used to define the *initial value* of **tf.Variable,** which itself defines both the shape and data type of the tensor.

In regards to a neural network, the initial values of all weights between the **network_input** and hidden **layer_1** are sampled from a random distribution.

This is accomplished by feeding **tf.random_normal's** *shape* argument two inputs: **784** and **layer_1_nodes.** With respect to a neural network, this *shape* defines the total number of connections between **network_input** nodes and **layer_1** nodes, and each connection requires a weight. Thus, it defines the total number of weights within the specified region.

Tf.random_normal has a single required argument and five optional arguments with default values. All are listed below:

Required: The shape of the output tensor. In our case, this is **784 x 500.**
Defaults values:
- mean = 0.0
- stddev = 1.0
- dtype = tf.float32
- seed = None
- name = None

What is "784" and "layer_1_nodes" ?

"784" is the total number of input nodes found in **network_input,** while **"layer_1_nodes"** is the number of nodes in hidden layer 1, which is 500. Both of these specify the **tf.random_normal's** *shape* argument.

Summing Up Line 17:

Line 17 defines the quantity of weights in-between **network_input** and **layer_1**. It also defines the initial values of each weight. Nonzero weights are important because weights, along with biases, are parameters that the network will adjust as it trains.

All of the weights are held in a tensor that is created using the **tf.Variable** class in combination with the **tf.random_normal** operation. The tensor has a shape of **784** x **500**, and it is this shape that defines the total number of weights.

Line 18

This line is almost identical to Line 17:

```
18. layer_1_bias =
tf.Variable(tf.random_normal([layer_1_nodes]))
```

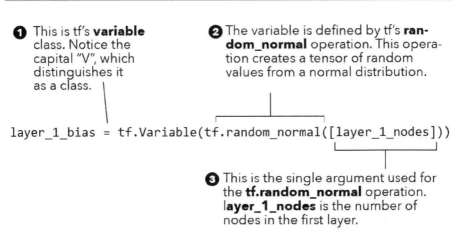

❶ This is tf's **variable** class. Notice the capital "V", which distinguishes it as a class.

❷ The variable is defined by tf's **random_normal** operation. This operation creates a tensor of random values from a normal distribution.

```
layer_1_bias = tf.Variable(tf.random_normal([layer_1_nodes]))
```

❸ This is the single argument used for the **tf.random_normal** operation. **layer_1_nodes** is the number of nodes in the first layer.

What is Line 18 accomplishing ?

Line 18 defines the quantity of adjustable parameters for **layer_1**. These parameters are the biases that sit on every edge, or connection, between each node in network_input and node in hidden layer_1. Line 18 also defines how the initial values of each parameter will be generated.

Note: in most neural networks the bias has a continuous output of 1. Hence, the final input a node receives from a bias is simply the value of the weight on the bias' connecting edge. For more on this, please see our math section.

As you can see, all of the elements in line 17 are found in line 18 *except* **784.** This means the shape of the tensor is based solely on **layer_1_nodes**, which is 500. Note that **tf.zeros** is often used in place of **tf.random_normal. tf.zeros** is an operation that creates a tensor with all elements set to 0 (zero). Each operation has pros and cons, and we have opted to use the former.

Summing Up Line 18:
Line 18 defines the quantity of bias connections for **layer_1,** which corresponds to the total number of bias weights. Line 18 also defines how the initial values of each bias will be generated, which is randomly.

All of these parameters are held in a tensor created using the **tf.Variable** class. The shape of the tensor defines the total number of bias values, which are sampled from the **tf.random_normal** operation.

Lines 19-24.
The remaining lines of code from line 19 - 24 are almost identical to those we have just analyzed, save that the arguments within **tf.random_normal** change. These changes occur because we are moving through the network layers, and the shape/number of weights and biases is always impacted by the previous layer.

Before moving onto Step 3's feedforward calculations, let's take a look at our code so far:

```
1. import tensorflow as tf
2. from tensorflow.examples.tutorials.mnist import
input_data
3. mnist = input_data.read_data_sets("/tmp/data/",
one_hot=True)
4.
5. learning_rate = 0.0001
6. batch_size = 100
7. update_step = 10
8.
9. layer_1_nodes = 500
10. layer_2_nodes = 500
11. layer_3_nodes = 500
12. output_nodes = 10
13.
14. network_input = tf.placeholder(tf.float32, [None, 784])
15. target_output = tf.placeholder(tf.float32, [None,
output_nodes])
16.
17. layer_1 = tf.Variable(tf.random_normal([784,
layer_1_nodes]))
```

```
18. layer_1_bias =
tf.Variable(tf.random_normal([layer_1_nodes]))
19. layer_2 = tf.Variable(tf.random_normal([layer_1_nodes,
layer_2_nodes]))
20. layer_2_bias =
tf.Variable(tf.random_normal([layer_2_nodes]))
21. layer_3 = tf.Variable(tf.random_normal([layer_2_nodes,
layer_3_nodes]))
22. layer_3_bias =
tf.Variable(tf.random_normal([layer_3_nodes]))
23. out_layer = tf.Variable(tf.random_normal([layer_3_nodes,
output_nodes]))
24. out_layer_bias =
tf.Variable(tf.random_normal([output_nodes]))
```

FeedForward Calculations

Since we have defined the shape and values of all weights and biases, we can now begin to add the mathematical calculations needed to move our inputs through the network. To do this, we will be using the ReLu activation function and a matrix multiplication operation.

Here is what we will be doing in code:
*Note: To make the code fit on a single line, we have shortened **"layer"** to the letter **"l"**. Reading code on a Kindle is difficult enough without it stretching across multiple lines.*

```
26. l1_output = tf.nn.relu(tf.matmul(network_input, layer_1)
+ layer_1_bias)
27. l2_output = tf.nn.relu(tf.matmul(l1_output, layer_2) +
layer_2_bias)
28. l3_output = tf.nn.relu(tf.matmul(l2_output, layer_3) +
layer_3_bias)
29. ntwk_output_1 = tf.matmul(l3_output, out_layer) +
out_layer_bias
30. ntwk_output_2 = tf.nn.softmax(ntwk_output_1)
```

Line 26

We will begin with assessing line 26, which will help you understand how lines 27 and 28 also work.

```
26. l1_output = tf.nn.relu(tf.matmul(network_input, layer_1)
+ layer_1_bias)
```

Line 26 is long, so we will break it into two sections:

Line 26: Section 1:

① **tf.nn.relu** is tf's ReLu activation operation. It is one of many activation functions available.

```
l1_output = tf.nn.relu
```

Line 26: Section 2:

② The Relu operation is applied to the output of **tf.matmul,** which is tf's matrix multiplication operation.

③ These are the two arguments used for the **tf.matmul** operation. We defined **network_input** in Step 2 and **layer_1** in Step 3.

```
(tf.matmul(network_input, layer_1) + layer_1_bias)
```

④ **layer_1_bias** is added to the outcome of the **matmul** operation. We defined **layer_1_bias** earlier in this step.

What is Line 26 Accomplishing?

Line 26 calculates the output of every node in the first hidden layer. It accomplishes this by applying the **tf.nn.relu** activation function to the output of **tf.matmul** summed with **layer_1_bias**. A total of two arguments are used for the **tf.matmul** operation.

What is tf.nn.relu ?

Tf.nn.relu is one of the 10 activation functions that Tensorflow offers, such as **tf.sigmoid** and **tf.tanh.** It is an operation that produces a tensor, and it requires a single argument, features, and also has an optional name argument. **Features** must be a certain type of tensor, such as float32 or float64. In our case, features are defined by the product of **tf.matmul** summed with **layer_1_bias.** For more in-depth information on activation functions, please see our math section.

What are "network_input" and "layer_1" ?

Both **network_input** and **layer_1** are arguments used to create the tensor that **tf.matmul** requires. We have already defined both of these back in Steps 2 and 3, respectively.

```
- network_input = tf.placeholder(tf.float32, [None, 784])
- layer_1 = tf.Variable(tf.random_normal([784,
layer_1_nodes]))
```

What is "layer_1_bias" ?

We defined **layer_1_bias** in Step 2, and in this context in simply "jiggles" the weighted inputs that are fed into the matmul operation.

```
- layer_1_bias =
tf.Variable(tf.random_normal([layer_1_nodes]))
```

Layer_1_bias is added to the output of **tf.matmul,** and the result is applied to the **tf.nn.relu** activation function.

Summing Up Line 26:

Line 26 is a result of numerous mathematical calculations, and we will work our way through these like a chain.

1. **L1_output** is the result of applying the **tf.nn.relu** activation function to each of **layer_1**'s weighted (and biased) inputs.
2. The value of each node is calculated by multiplying each input by a weight and summing, using **tf.matmul,** then adding each node's bias to the result.
3. The **tf.matmul** operation takes two arguments, the **network_input** and **layer_1.** We know that **network_input** is a vector of 784 values (a 784D tensor representing input nodes), and that **layer_1** is tensor that feeds into 500 nodes.

As you can tell by looking at the code a few pages back, **l2_output** and **l3_output** are calculated in the same fashion as **l1_output.** The only differences are the changing biases and arguments, which is because the inputs to each layer change, along with the biases.

Let's move on to Lines 29 and 30, which are likely somewhat confounding. Why are there two outputs being calculated ? We'll discover the answer in a moment.

```
29. ntwk_output_1 = tf.matmul(l3_output, out_layer) +
out_layer_bias
30. ntwk_output_2 = tf.nn.softmax(ntwk_output_1)
```

Line 29
Let's start with Line 29.

```
29. ntwk_output_1 = tf.matmul(l3_output, out_layer) +
out_layer_bias
```

Line 29 is long, so we will divide it into two sections.

Line 29: Section 1:

❶ This is the same **tf.matmul** operation we saw earlier on line 26 .

```
ntwk_output_1 = tf.matmul
```

Line 29: Section 2:

❷ These are the two arguments used for the **tf.matmul** operation. We defined **l3_output** and **out_layer** a few pages back.

```
(l3_output, out_layer) + out_layer_bias
```

❸ **out_layer_bias** is added to the outcome of the **matmul** operation. We defined **out_layer_bias** earlier in this step.

What is Line 29 accomplishing ?

Line 29 is calculating the final output of the network, but the output is not put through an activation function as in previous layers. Technically this output is called a **logit,** or **logits,** and will be required for when we use the **cross-entropy** cost function in Step 4.

What is "tf.matmul" ?

As you already know, **tf.matmul** is a Tensorflow operation that multiplies two matrices together. The input to it must either be matrices or tensors that are => 2-dimensional. In our case, the input is composed of two arguments, **l3_output** and **out_layer,** and both are tensors.

What is "l3_output" and "out_layer" ?

L3_output is the last hidden layer and **out_layer** is used to compute the output logits. Both of these are tensors that we defined previously: **out_layer** in Step 2 and **l3_output** earlier in our current step.

What is "out_layer_bias" ?

This is a tensor that has already been discussed and defined earlier in this step.

Summing Up Line 29:

The unscaled output of the network, **ntwk_output_1,** is a result of numerous mathematical calculations:

> 1.The **tf.matmul** operation is applied to two arguments, which are **l3_output** and **out_layer.** We know that **l3_output** is a tensor that contains 500 nodes, and that **out_layer_weights** is a matrix tensor that feeds into 10 nodes.

2. The **out_layer_bias** is added to the result of each **tf.matmul** operation for each output layer node (10 total). After this, the final (unscaled) output of each output node are the output logits.

Line 30

Finally, let's look at Line 30!

```
30. ntwk_output_2 = tf.nn.softmax(ntwk_output_1)
```

---

❶ **tf.nn.softmax** is tf's Softmax activation operation. It is one of many activation functions available for classification. It is applied to **ntwk_output_1**.

```
ntwk_output_2 = tf.nn.softmax(ntwk_output_1)
```

❷ We just defined **ntwk_output_1** on line 30. It is the unfiltered output of the network.

What is Line 30 accomplishing ?

Line 30 calculates the 0-1 probabilities from the final output of the network by putting the logits through the softmax activation function. This is in contrast to the raw numbers from Line 29 directly above. Line 30 will be used to calculate the **correct prediction** and **accuracy** of our network as we move forward.

What is "tf.nn.softmax" ?

tf.nn.softmax is an activation function that is specifically used for classification. Tensorflow offers a variety of classification operations, but softmax is quite popular for a variety of reasons.

Tf.nn.softmax has a single required argument and two arguments with default values *which can be changed, but are not required to be.* In our case, the required argument is **ntwk_output_1**, and the other two arguments are default values:

Required: Logits, which must be a tensor with a data type of *half, float32, or float64.* In our case, we calculated the logits with **ntwk_output_1**.

Defaults values:
- dim = -1
- name = None

What is "ntwk_output_1" ?
We have already discussed and defined this on Line 29.

Summing Up Line 30:
The scaled output of the network, **ntwk_output_2**, is arrived at by applying a **softmax** activation function to the unscaled output, **ntwk_output_1**.

Our code up until this point is as follows:

```
1. import tensorflow as tf
2. from tensorflow.examples.tutorials.mnist import
input_data
3. mnist = input_data.read_data_sets("/tmp/data/",
one_hot=True)
4.
5. learning_rate = 0.0001
6. batch_size = 100
7. update_step = 10
8.
9. layer_1_nodes = 500
10. layer_2_nodes = 500
11. layer_3_nodes = 500
12. output_nodes = 10
13.
14. network_input = tf.placeholder(tf.float32, [None, 784])
15. target_output = tf.placeholder(tf.float32, [None,
output_nodes])
16.
17. layer_1 = tf.Variable(tf.random_normal([784,
layer_1_nodes]))
18. layer_1_bias =
tf.Variable(tf.random_normal([layer_1_nodes]))
19. layer_2 = tf.Variable(tf.random_normal([layer_1_nodes,
layer_2_nodes]))
20. layer_2_bias =
tf.Variable(tf.random_normal([layer_2_nodes]))
```

```
21. layer_3 = tf.Variable(tf.random_normal([layer_2_nodes,
layer_3_nodes]))
22. layer_3_bias =
tf.Variable(tf.random_normal([layer_3_nodes]))
23. out_layer = tf.Variable(tf.random_normal([layer_3_nodes,
output_nodes]))
24. out_layer_bias =
tf.Variable(tf.random_normal([output_nodes]))
25.
26. l1_output = tf.nn.relu(tf.matmul(network_input, layer_1)
+ layer_1_bias)
27. l2_output = tf.nn.relu(tf.matmul(l1_output, layer_2) +
layer_2_bias)
28. l3_output = tf.nn.relu(tf.matmul(l2_output, layer_3) +
layer_3_bias)
29. ntwk_output_1 = tf.matmul(l3_output, out_layer) +
out_layer_bias
30. ntwk_output_2 = tf.nn.softmax(ntwk_output_1)
```

Step 4: Define Training Elements

In the fourth step, various elements are defined that are necessary to train the network, including the network's prediction, cost function, optimization function and training step .

Here is everything we will be doing in code:
Note: we have shortened more natural and 'intuitive' names in order for the code to fit better on a Kindle. We will explain each in detail further on.

```
32. cf =
tf.reduce_mean(tf.nn.softmax_cross_entropy_with_logits(logi
ts=ntwk_output_1, labels=target_output))

33. ts =
tf.train.GradientDescentOptimizer(learning_rate).minimize(c
f)
34. cp = tf.equal(tf.argmax(ntwk_output_2, 1),
tf.argmax(target_output, 1))
35. acc = tf.reduce_mean(tf.cast(cp, tf.float32))
```

Line 32

```
cf =
tf.reduce_mean(tf.nn.softmax_cross_entropy_with_logits(logi
ts=ntwk_output_1, labels=target_output))
```

This line is large, so we will break it into 2 sections.

Line 32: Section 1:

❶ **tf.reduce_mean** is a tf operation that reduces various dimensions of a tensor. It is one of many tf reduction operations available.

```
cf = tf.reduce_mean(tf.nn.softmax_cross_entropy_with_logits
```

❷ **tf.reduce_mean** is applied to the output of **tf.nn.softmax**... Read below for more details.

Line 32: Section 2:

❶ This is the first argument used for the **tf.softmax**... operation. It defines logits as **ntwk_output_1**, which we defined in Step 3.

```
(logits=ntwk_output_1, labels=target_output))
```

❷ This is the second argument used for the **tf.nn.softmax** operation. It defines labels as **target_output**, which we defined in Step 2.

What is Line 32 accomplishing ?

Line 32 computes the cost (or loss, or error) of the network. This is why we have named it **cf**, for cost function.

It accomplishes this by applying **tf.reduce_mean** to the output of the **tf.nn.softmax...** operation. Within the **tf.nn.softmax...** operation, the cross-entropy cost function is applied *to the output of* the softmax activation function; to successfully accomplish this, two arguments are required: logits and labels.

What is "tf.reduce_mean" ?

Tf.reduce_mean is a tf operation that computes the mean value(s) of a tensor, while reducing its dimensionality (rank). If you recall from our introduction, a tensor is a multidimensional array. **Tf.reduce_mean** is used to reduce one or more of these dimensions. Tensorflow also offers various other reduction operations, such as **tf.reduce_sum** and **tf.reduce_max**.

Practically speaking, **tf.reduce_mean** calculates the average, or mean, of elements across dimensions of a tensor. It accomplishes this by reducing the required *input tensor* along the lines of the *axis*. Within this context, an *axis* is a specific dimension, and if no specific axis is given as an argument, all of the tensors dimensions are reduced to 1. See tensorflow.org for more information.

Tf.reduce_mean has a single required argument and four optional arguments with default values.

Required: input tensor
Default values:
- *axis = None*
- *keep_dims = False*
- *reduction_indices = None*
- *name = None*

What is "tf.nn.softmax_cross_entropy_with_logits" ?

Tf.nn.softmax... is a tf operation that performs two tasks in one.

1. It applies the **softmax** activation function to the *net input* of every output node in a network. The result is a new network output that has been put through an activation function. To do this it uses **ntwk_output_1.**

2. It applies the **cross_entropy** cost function to the new output it generated above. The end result is the discovery of the network's

error (or cost, or loss). To do this, it uses **logits** found in **target_output**.

What is "logits = ntwk_output_1" ?
Logits is the first required argument for **tf.nn.softmax...** Logits are the output of all output layer nodes *without going through an activation function*. Technically, this makes them the *net input* of all output layer nodes.

We **ntwk_output_1** as the **logits,** and we calculated this in Step 3.

What is "labels = target_output" ?
Labels are the second required argument for **tf.nn.softmax...** Labels are the target output of every training image, which is **target_output.** This is a tf Variable, which is a tensor, and we defined it in Step 2.

Summing Up Line 32:
Line 32 computes the error of the network, which is commonly called the "cost". It accomplishes this by applying **tf.reduce_mean** to the output of the **tf.nn.softmax...** operation.

Line 33

```
33. ts =
tf.train.GradientDescentOptimizer(learning_rate).minimize(c
f)
```

Line 33: Section 1:

❶ **tf.train.Grad...** is a tf subclass of the Optimizer class that performs gradient descent. It is one of many optimizers available.

```
ts = tf.train.GradientDescentOptimizer(learning_rate)
```

❷ This is the single argument used for the **tf.train.Grad..** sublcass. It makes use of **learning_rate**, which we defined in Step 2.

Line 33: Section 2:

❶ .minimize is a tf method that minimizes the
cost(loss) computed by the optimizer.

```
            |
   .minimize(cf)
```

What is Line 33 accomplishing ?
Line 33 defines the training step, which is the size of step (or distance)
that the network will take towards minimizing the cost function (**cf**).
Hence, we have named this **ts.**

Practically speaking, this occurs by minimizing the cost function
(**.minimize**) through gradient descent (**tf.train.Grad....**) while
making use of the learning rate (**learning_rate).**

What is "tf.train.GradientDescentOptimizer" ?
Tf.train.Grad.... is a subclass of the Optimizer class, and it applies the
gradient descent algorithm to the weights and biases. It has a single
required argument, which is the learning rate. It also has two optional
default argument values, which you might see in other code examples:
- use_locking = False
- name = GradientDescent

For more on gradient descent, please see our math section.

What is "learning_rate" ?
We already defined this in Step 2.

What is ".minimize" ?
Minimize is a Tensorflow method that minimizes the error, or cost, of a
network. It has a single required argument and multiple optional
arguments with default values.

Required: The loss, or cost. This must be a tensor.
Default:
- global_step = None
- var_list = None
- gate_gradients = GATE_OP

- aggregation_method = None
- colocate_gradients_with_ops = False
- grad_loss = None
- name = None

Summing Up Line 33:

Line 33 defines the size of step that the network will take towards minimizing the cost function (**cf**). This is often called the "training step", which is why it is abbreviated as **ts.**

On a practical level, this occurs by minimizing the cost function (**.minimize**) through gradient descent (**tf.train.Grad....**) while making use of the learning rate (**learning_rate**).

Line 34

```
34. cp = tf.equal(tf.argmax(ntwk_output_2, 1),
tf.argmax(target_output, 1))
```

We will break this into two sections:

Line 34: Section 1

❶ **tf.equal** is a tf operation that returns a truth value of x == y. It uses two arguments to accomlish this, and it outputs "true" or "false".

```
cp = tf.equal(tf.argmax
```

❷ **tf.argmax** is a tf operation that returns the index of the largest value aross the axes of a tensor. This wil be explained in more detail below.

Line 34: Section 2

❶ ntwrk_output_2 is the first argument used for the first **tf.argmax** operation. We defined this in Step 3.

```
(ntwrk_output_2, 1), tf.argmax(target_output_, 1))
```

❷ "1" is used to define the **axis**, which is the second argument for both **tf.argmax** operations. This will be explored more below.

What is Line 34 accomplishing ?

Line 34 evaluates which predictions of the network are correct, hence its name, **cp.** It accomplishes this by using **tf.argmax** in conjunction with **tf.equal** to check if the network's predictions and labels are a match. In other words, it answers the question: which predictions did the network get right ?

What is "tf.equal" ?

Tf.equal is a tf operation that returns a truth value when given two arguments, **a** and **b.** Practically speaking, this means that it checks whether the network prediction for an image matches the correct target *label* for the image. It asks the question *does the actual output match the target output ?* If you recall, labels were defined in Step 2 as **target_output.**

Tf.equal compares two arguments, both of which are required. A third default value argument is optional:

Required: a, b.
Default:
- name = None

Both required arguments, **a** and **b,** must be tensors of the same type. In our case, the two tensors are defined by **tf.argmax.**

What is "tf.argmax" ?

The official definition: "**Tf.argmax** is a tf operation that returns the index with the largest value across axes of a tensor". This is complex, so we will break it apart and explain it in terms of a neural network:

1. Every output node in **ntwk_output_2** has an index position and value. The index position is the node's position within an array, corresponding to that classification (3 for numeral "3" etc.). The value is a variable, which is the product of applying an activation function, representing the probability that the input has that classification.
1. The output node with the highest value is considered the network's "prediction". The **tf.argmax** operation finds this maximum and returns the index position of that value as its output.

To dig deeper, here are a few more points to consider.

Point 1: Definitions
- A tensor is a multidimensional array.
- An axis refers to either a row or column.
- An index is the position of a value along an axis.

Point 2: The Axis Argument
The arrays of a tensor can be assessed two ways: by row or column. The **axis** argument enables Tensorflow to select which way, row or column, and then assess all arrays via that method. If **axis** is not provided, the **argmax** operation flattens the entire tensor into a single row.

- axis = 0. This finds the maximum within the columns of every array in the tensor.
- axis = 1. This finds the maximum within the rows of every array in the tensor.

In our case, we define the axis as **1.**

Point 3: Arguments
We use **tf.argmax** twice to generate the arguments necessary for **tf.equal,** and in both cases we provide **tf.argmax** with two arguments. These arguments are **input** and **axis,** and they will be discussed further below.

The first use of **tf.argmax** analyzes the values of every single output node found in **ntwk_output_2.** Each output node has an index, and the **tf.argmax** operation outputs the index of the node with the highest value.

The second use of **tf.argmax** analyzes the values of every single node found in **target_output**. Again, each node has an index, and **tf.argmax** outputs the index of the node with the highest value.

These outputs then become the arguments for the **tf.equal** operation, and a verdict of *true or false* is given.

Tf.argmax requires a single argument and contains three optional default arguments.

Required: input.
Default:
- *axis = None*
- *name = None*
- *dimension = None*

What is "ntwk_output_2, target_output and 1" ?
Ntwk_output_2 and **target_output** were defined in Step 2. With respect to Line 34, both of these are used to fulfill the required *input* argument for each **tf.argmax** operation. **"1"** is the **axis** argument, and it tells Tensorflow to assess all of its arrays by rows, not columns.

Line 35:
Now we will examine Line 35:

```
35. acc = tf.reduce_mean(tf.cast(cp, tf.float32))
```

❶ **tf.reduce_mean** is a tf operation that is applied to the output of **tf.cast**. We already examined **tf.reduce_mean** earlier in Step 4.

```
acc = tf.reduce_mean(tf.cast(cp, tf.float32))
```

❷ **tf.cast** is a tf operation that changes the type of a tensor. It requires two arguments.

❸ These are the two arguments used for the **tf.cast** operation. We have defined/examined both previously.

What is Line 35 accomplishing ?

Line 35 finds the average number of correct predictions from Line 34. If you recall, the output of Line 34 is simply an array of *true* and *false* statements. Line 35 takes this array and changes its values to floating point numbers, and then takes the mean of all those numbers.

Taking the mean is accomplished by applying the **tf.reduce_mean** operation to the output of the **tf.cast** operation.

What is "tf.reduce_mean" ?

We already defined this in previous steps. In this instance, it is applied to the output of **tf.cast.**

What is "tf.cast" ?

Tf.cast is a tf operation that alters the datatype of a tensor. In our case, it is changing the *true/false* values of **cp** to floating point numbers.

Tf.cast requires two arguments, and has a third optional default argument.
Required:
*- x = an input tensor. In our case, this is **cp**.*
*- dtype = datatype. This is the datatype that the input tensor will be changed to. In our case, this is **tf.float32**.*

What is "cp" and "tf.float32" ?

Both of these have been defined in previous steps.

We are now finished with Step 4, and will be bridging into Part 2. Our code up until now is as follows:

```
1. import tensorflow as tf
2. from tensorflow.examples.tutorials.mnist import
input_data
3. mnist = input_data.read_data_sets("/tmp/data/",
one_hot=True)
4.
5. learning_rate = 0.0001
6. batch_size = 100
7. update_step = 10
8.
9. layer_1_nodes = 500
```

```
10. layer_2_nodes = 500
11. layer_3_nodes = 500
12. output_nodes = 10
13.
14. network_input = tf.placeholder(tf.float32, [None, 784])
15. target_output = tf.placeholder(tf.float32, [None,
output_nodes])
16.
17. layer_1 = tf.Variable(tf.random_normal([784,
layer_1_nodes]))
18. layer_1_bias =
tf.Variable(tf.random_normal([layer_1_nodes]))
19. layer_2 = tf.Variable(tf.random_normal([layer_1_nodes,
layer_2_nodes]))
20. layer_2_bias =
tf.Variable(tf.random_normal([layer_2_nodes]))
21. layer_3 = tf.Variable(tf.random_normal([layer_2_nodes,
layer_3_nodes]))
22. layer_3_bias =
tf.Variable(tf.random_normal([layer_3_nodes]))
23. out_layer = tf.Variable(tf.random_normal([layer_3_nodes,
output_nodes]))
24. out_layer_bias =
tf.Variable(tf.random_normal([output_nodes]))
25.
26. l1_output = tf.nn.relu(tf.matmul(network_input, layer_1)
+ layer_1_bias)
27. l2_output = tf.nn.relu(tf.matmul(l1_output, layer_2) +
layer_2_bias)
28. l3_output = tf.nn.relu(tf.matmul(l2_output, layer_3) +
layer_3_bias)
29. ntwk_output_1 = tf.matmul(l3_output, out_layer) +
out_layer_bias
30. ntwk_output_2 = tf.nn.softmax(ntwk_output_1)
31.
32. cf =
tf.reduce_mean(tf.nn.softmax_cross_entropy_with_logits(logi
ts=ntwk_output_1, labels=target_output))
33. ts =
tf.train.GradientDescentOptimizer(learning_rate).minimize(c
f)
```

```
34. cp = tf.equal(tf.argmax(ntwk_output_2, 1),
tf.argmax(target_output, 1))
35. acc = tf.reduce_mean(tf.cast(cp, tf.float32))
```

Part 2: Running the Tensorflow Graph

Step 5: Create a Session

The next step in building a network is to create a session object. This session will run the computational graph we created in Steps 2-4. Inside of the session, we will create a loop that trains the network and prints update statements to our screen. A final accuracy statement will also be printed when training is complete. Let's begin.

We will be producing the following code in this Step:
Note: To help with indentation levels, we have marked each line with the following:

███████████████████████

```python
37. with tf.Session() as sess:
38.     sess.run(tf.global_variables_initializer())
39.      num_epochs = 10
40.     for epoch in range(num_epochs):
41.         total_cost = 0
42.          for _ in range(int(mnist.train.num_examples /
batch_size)):
43.                 batch_x, batch_y =
mnist.train.next_batch(batch_size)
44.                 t, c = sess.run([ts, cf],
feed_dict={network_input: batch_x, target_output: batch_y})
45.             total_cost += c
46.             print('Epoch', epoch, 'completed out of',
num_epochs, 'loss:', total_cost)
47.     print('Accuracy:', acc.eval({network_input:
mnist.test.images, target_output: mnist.test.labels}))
```

We will begin by examining Line 37.

Line 37:

███████████████████████

37. `with tf.Session() as sess:`

---

❶ This uses Python's **"with"** statement to create a **tf.Session** object. Notice the capital **"S"**, which denotes a class. The session will automatically close once all of its nested code is complete.

`with tf.Session() as sess:`

❷ Python's **"as"** keyword is used to rename the object to **sess**.

What is Line 37 accomplishing ?

Line 37 is quite straightforward. It creates a **tf.Session** object that will enable us to run our network (or computational graph, as it is called in Tensorflow) - and it renames the object as **sess.** Remember, in Steps 1-4 we created our graph and defined our computations. Now, we are going to execute the graph.

The remaining code (lines 38 - 47) will all be nested underneath Line 38.

Line 38:

███████████████████

---

38. `sess.run(tf.global_variables_initializer())`

---

❶ Tensorflow's **.run** method is used to invovlk the session object, **sess.**

`sess.run(tf.global_variables_initializer())`

❷ This argument is a tf operation that initializes all global variables in the tf graph.

What is Line 38 accomplishing ?

Line 38 essentially "turns the key" and starts the engine of the computational graph by initializing all the global variables we have defined. It accomplishes this by invoking the session object created on Line 37 with tf's **run** method.

What is ".run" ?

.run is a tensorflow method that runs an operation and evaluates tensors. It requires a single argument and has a number of optional default arguments.

Required: fetches. Fetches can be a list, tuple, dictionary, etc. In our case, it is a Tensorflow function.
Default:
- feed_dict = None.
- options = None
- run_metadata = None

What is "tf.global_variables_initializer" ?
Tf.global_variables_initializer is a tensorflow function that initializes all global variables in our graph. Global variables are created with the **tf.Variable** class. In our case, our global variables are located on Lines 17 - 24.

Tf.global_variables_initializer requires a single argument, which is a list of variables. It also has an optional default name argument.

Line 39:

```
39.    num_epochs = 10
```

❶ **num_epochs** is a Python variable that defines the amount of epochs that the network will train for.

```
num_epochs = 10
```

What is Line 39 accomplishing ?
Line 39 is a variable that defines the total number of times the network will cycle through all of its training dataset, and is used in a loop on Line 40.

Line 40:

```
40.    for epoch in range(num_epochs):
```

① Python's **range** function is used to create a loop that will run
through all of the code nested underneath it x times. The term
"epoch" is arbitrary, and could be anything.

```
for epoch in range(num_epochs):
```

② **"num_epochs"** is the single
argument used for the range
function. It tells the loop to run 10
times.

What is Line 40 accomplishing ?

Line 40 creates a loop that defines how many epochs our network will
train for. Remember, an epoch is when an entire training set *goes
forward and backward* through the network. As you can see, our network
will train for 10 epochs. *Note: the term **epoch** could be anything, but we
feel it is intuitive.*

Line 41:

```
41.            total_cost = 0
```

This line is easy to understand and thus we will not magnify it and break
it down. It defines the total cost, and every time an epoch is completed,
the cost will be updated. This cost, or loss, represents the total error of the
network, and our goal is to minimize it. *Note: the term **total_cost** could
be anything, but we feel it is intuitive.*

Line 42:

```
42.            for _ in range(int(mnist.train.num_examples /
batch_size)):
```

❶ Python's **range** function is used to create a loop within a loop (line 41). This new loop will run through all of the code nested underneath it. Its range is defined by python's **int** function.

```
for _ in range(int(mnist.train.num_examples / batch_size)):
```

❷ This is the single argument used for the range function. It divides **training examples** by **batch_size**. Read more below.

What is Line 42 accomplishing ?

Line 42 defines the number of batches in a single epoch, and then uses this value to create a loop using Python's **range** function. As you will see on Lines 43-45, this loop will iterate over every single batch in an epoch, and every time it iterates, it will load a new, fresh batch of images and train the network to give more correct answers.

The fresh images will be fed into the **network_input** placeholder we created, while their corresponding target answers will be fed into the **target_output** placeholder. This is what we promised the network on Lines 14 and 15.

Note that Line 42 is a loop within a loop, and will execute all of its nested code a total of 10 times.

What is "_" ?

"_" stands for a variable that we are not concerned with. It is common to use _ , but it could literally be any other letter or term. We have chosen to use _.

What is "int" ?

Int is a Python function that converts a string or number to an integer. In our case, it takes the result of its argument (a division equation) and converts it to an integer. The result is then used to create a looping range.

Int requires a single argument and has an optional default value arguments. In our example, it makes use of two inputs for its required argument.

Required: X. This must be a number or string.
Default:
-    base = 10

-

What is "mnist.train.num_examples" ?
Mnist.train is an instance of the class **DataSet,** which we imported via
input_data on Line 2. **Num_examples** is a variable in that class, and
mnist_train.num_examples is simply the total number of training
examples.

Although not important for our code, the following is also true:
- mnist.validation.num_examples = total number of validation examples.
- mnist.test.num_examples = total number of testing examples.

What is "batch_size" ?
We defined **batch_size** in Part 2. It is 100.

Line 43:

```
43.                    batch_x, batch_y =
mnist.train.next_batch(batch_size)
```

❶ **Batch_x** represents input data, and **batch_y** represents labels.
These variables are essentially batches of images and correct
answers that we will iterate over. The names **batch_x** and **batch_y**
are changeable.

```
batch_x, batchch_y = mnist.train.next_batch(batch_size)
```

❷ This defines next_batch as **batch_size,** which
we defined in Step 2 and is 100.

What is Line 43 accomplishing ?
Line 43 defines two variables, **batch_x** and **batch_y.** For each training
iteration (defined by **int** on Line 44), 100 new, fresh training examples
are loaded into each variable. **Batch _x** receives 100 training examples,
while **batch_y** receives the corresponding target for each example.

What are "batch_x" and "batch_y" ?
"Batch_x" and "batch_y" have already been explained. They are
variables that receive "batches" of fresh training examples and target

outputs. Both names are arbitrary and could be altered. However, we find both intuitive.

What is "mnist.train.next_batch" ?
Mnist.train is an instance of the class **DataSet,** while **next_batch** is a method of the same class (we loaded the class on Line 2 via **input_data).** Together, **mnist.train.next_batch** fills **batch_x** and **batch_y** with the data they require (see above). It accomplishes this by using **batch_size.**

What is "batch_size" ?
We defined this in Step 2. It is 100.

Line 44:

```
44.                     t, c = sess.run([ts, cf],
feed_dict={network_input: batch_x, target_output: batch_y})
```

Line 44 is long, so we will break it into two sections:

Line 44: Section 1

❶ Tensorflow's **.run** method is used to involk the session object, **sess.**

❸ These two operations compose **.run's** **fetches** argument.

```
t, c = sess.run([ts, cf],
```

❷ **"t"** represents training step, while **"c"** represents cost. We will explore these more below.

Line 44: Section 2

❶ Feed_dict is a second argument for the **.run** method, and it is a dictionary that we fill, or feed. We fill it with two keys and their respective values.

```
feed_dict={network_input: batch_x, target_output: batch_y})
```

❷ network_input is a key, while **batch_x** is its value.

❸ target_output is a key, while **batch_y** is its value.

What is Line 44 accomplishing ?
Line 44 feeds the fresh batches we generated on Line 43 into the placeholders we defined in Step 2: **network_input** and **target_output**. These batches are technically fed into a dictionary via **feed_dict**, and then both the training step, **ts**, and cost function, **cf**, are evaluated on each batch.

This process repeats itself for each epoch (10 total) until all batches have been processed.

What are "t" and "c" ?
Both are variables that hold the temporary values created by the session's operations, **ts** and **cf**.
"T" stands for training step, while **"c"** stand for cost function. We will not be using **"t"** for anything specific, but we will make use of **"c"** to update the network cost on Line 45.

What is ".run" ?
We already defined **.run** on Line 38.

What are "ts" and "cf" ?
"Ts" is the training step and **"cf"** is the cost function We defined these in Step 3.

What is "feed_dict" ?
Feed_dict is a tf argument that allows you to supply, or feed, data to a tensor. This new information is fed into a dictionary (basically a lookup table), hence its name! In our case, we are feeding batches of 100 images

and their target outputs into two tensors: **network_input** and **target_output.**

Remember, both of these tensors are placeholders *waiting* for information, which we are now finally giving to them. We defined both placeholders in Part 2.

What are "network_input" and "batch_x" ?
This is the first key-value pair of the **feed_dict** argument.
Network_input is the key, and it is the empty placeholder we created in Step 2. **Batch_x** is the fresh batch of training images we just created on Line 43.

What are "target_output" and "batch_y" ?
This is the second key-value pair of the **feed_dict** argument.
Target_output is the key, and it is the empty placeholder we created in Step 2. **Batch_y** is the fresh batch of target output labels we just created on Line 43.

Line 45:

```
45.                     total_cost += c
```

1 **Total_cost** is the error of the network. We defined this on Line 42.

```
  ┌───┴───┐
total_cost += c
            └─┬─┘
              │
```

2 This operation adds **c** to **total cost.** It is the same as **total_cost = total_cost + c.**

What is Line 45 accomplishing ?
This line is straightforward. It updates the **total_cost** of the network by adding the new cost, **c,** from Line 44.

Line 46:

```
46.        print('Epoch', epoch, 'completed out of 10
epochs.',num_epochs 'Total Loss:', total_cost)
```

What is Line 46 accomplishing ?

This line is also easy to understand and thus we will not magnify it and break it down. It is simply printing an update for every epoch. This update includes the current **epoch** and **total_cost**, both of which we have defined earlier in this step.

Line 47:

```
47.        print('Accuracy:', acc.eval({network_input:
mnist.test.images, target_output: mnist.test.labels}))
```

This line is complex. We will break it into sections.

Line 47: Section 1

❶ This line tells Python to print the word **Accuracy**, along with an evaluation of the networks accuracy, **acc**. It uses tf's **eval** method to do this.

```
print('Accuracy:', accuracy.eval
```

Line 47: Section 2

❶ This is the first key-value entry for **tf.eval's feed_dict** argument. **network_input** is a key, **mnist.test.images** is its value.

```
({network_input: mnist.test.images, target_output: mnist.test.labels}))
```

❷ This is the second key-value entry for **tf.eval's feed_dict** argument. **target_output** is a key, **mnist.test.labels** is its value.

What is Line 47 accomplishing ?

Line 47 prints the final accuracy of our network - but not based on training examples. Instead, once all epochs are complete, Line 47 runs 10,000 test images through the network. It is our network's ability to classify these 10,000 images that is represented in the final accuracy.

Line 47 accomplishes this by feeding test images and labels into the placeholders we defined in Step 2: **network_input** and **target_output**. This data is technically fed into a dictionary via **feed_dict**, and accuracy, **acc**, is performed on the data.

All of this is accomplished by launching a new session using tf's **eval** method, and passing an argument into the session.

What is "acc.eval" ?

"Acc" is a tensor that we defined in Step 4, and it stands for *accuracy*. **"Acc.eval"** launches a new session, and is equivalent to **sess.run(acc)**. **"Eval"** requires a single argument, which is **feed_dict,** and also has an optional **session** argument. In our case, **feed_dict** is fed with two key-value entries.

What is "network_input: mnist.test.images" ?

This is the first key-value entry for **eval's feed_dict** argument. **"Network_input"** is a key, and is one of the placeholders we defined in Step 2. **"Mnist.test.images"** is the key's value, and is defined via the **read_data_sets** method on Line 3.

What is "target_output: mnist.test.labels" ?

This is the second key-value entry for **eval's feed_dict** argument. **"Target_output"** is a key, and is also one of the placeholders we defined in Step 2. **"Mnist.test.labels"** is the key's value, and it too is defined via the **read_data_sets** method on Line 3.

Ch. 29

Classifying Images in 10 Minutes

10 minutes. That's all it takes to build an image classifier thanks to Google! In this chapter, we will provide a high-level overview of how to classify images using a convolutional neural network (CNN) and Google's Inception V3 model. Once finished, you will be able to tweak this code to classify any type of image sets! Cats, bats, super heroes - the sky's the limit.

This chapter is divided into the following sections:
1. Overview
2. Building the Classifier
3. Next Steps

Overview
In this chapter, we will retrain Google's Inception V3 to classify two sets of reptiles: snakes and lizards. To do this we will use Docker.

What is Inception?
Google's Inception is a deep convolutional neural network (CNN or ConvNet) that has been trained on a million images and can differentiate between 1,000 classes - and Google has made this available to anyone, anywhere!

The final "layer" of the deep CNN can be re-trained to classify new images. This is called *transfer-learning*, and it makes use of all of the information learned by the *lower layers* in the network. This is what we will be doing in this chapter. For more information on retraining, visit tensorflow.org.

What is Docker?
Docker's *Community Edition* is a free program that creates virtual environments, or containers, on your computer. It essentially removes the frustration and hassles of working on projects in different code and on

different operating systems. If a program is stored in Docker, it will work on any machine, regardless of its operating system, etc.

In our situation, using Docker eliminates the need to install tensorflow or any other dependencies - which means that all of us will be able to easily follow and work on this together. It doesn't matter if you are on a PC, Mac or have Python 2.7 or 3.5.

Building the Classifier:
There are 8 steps to building our classifier - and they are short!

Step 1: Install and Test Docker
Step 2: Create Container w/ TF Image
Step 3: Create Directories w/ Images
Step 4: Link Images to Docker TF Image
Step 5: Retrieve Training Code
Step 6: Retrain Inception
Step 7: Download Python Gist
Step 8: Classify

Step 1: Install and Test Docker
First, we need to install and test Docker. Go to docker.com and download Docker - and make sure you select the Community Edition! Follow the setup instructions and then test your installation.

To test your installation, open a command-line terminal. Then, launch a new docker container and run the hello-world image:

```
~$ docker run hello-world
```

If it works correctly, you should see something similar to the following:

```
Hello from Docker!
This message shows that your installation appears to be
working correctly.
```

Step 2: Create Container w/ TF Image
Next, we need to create a Docker container and load the Tensorflow image into the container. This will provide us with all of the dependencies we need to build our classifier - how fantastic is that ? We will do this in one line of code.

To launch a new container with the Tensorflow image, type the following into your command-line terminal:

```
~$ docker run -it gcr.io/tensorflow/tensorflow:latest-devel
```

If the above doesn't work, you might have to run docker using the *sudo* command. For example:

```
~$ sudo docker run -it gcr.io/tensorflow/tensorflow:latest-devel
```

You should see a new prompt similar to the following:

```
root@xxxxxxx#
```

If you see the above, you are in a new Docker container! Now, test the Tensorflow image by loading Python and importing Tensorflow.

```
~$ python
>>> import tensorflow as tf
>>>
```

If both Python and tensorflow successfully loaded, the image and container are working correctly.We are ready to move on.

To exit Python, type:

```
>>> quit()
```

To exit the docker container, press:

```
root@xxxxxxx#: ctrl-D
```

Step 3: Create Directories w/ Images
We now need to create a few directories that will store the images we will be classifying.
First, make sure you are at your default prompt. Type:

```
~$ cd $HOME
```

Next, create a directory called *tf_files*, and then open it to create another directory. For our example, we are classifying two different types of reptiles, and so we will name this second directory *reptiles*.

```
~$ mkdir tf_files
~$ cd tf_files
~ tf_files$ mkdir reptiles
```

Now, open *reptiles* and create two new directories, one for each group of images. For our example, we will use *snakes* and *lizards*.

```
~tf_files$ cd reptiles
~reptiles$ mkdir snakes
~reptiles$ mkdir lizards
```

Next, open *Finder* on Mac or *My Computer* on a PC. Find the folders *snakes* and *lizards* and transfer the images you are wanting to classify into each respective folder. The easiest way to do this is to "drag and drop" the images you download into their respective folders.

Step 4: Link Images to Docker TF Image
We now need to link the folder and images to our Docker container. This will enable Inception to re-train using our images. We can do this on a single line:

Back in terminal, make sure you are at your default prompt. Type:

```
~$ cd $HOME
```

Then type the following to link the *tf_files folder* and launch the container:

```
~$ docker run -it -v $HOME/tf_files:/tf_files
gcr.io/tensorflow/tensorflow:latest-devel
```

You should see a new prompt similar to the following:
```
root@xxxxxxx#
```

Now, to test if the images linked properly, type the following:

```
root@xxxxxxx# cd /tf_files
```

If *tf_files* opens, you are good to go! You can double-check by digging deeper typing to see if the directory *reptiles, etc.*, are also present.

Step 5: Retrieve Training Code
The next step is to retrieve the training code from Tensorflow. To do this, type the following:

```
root@xxxxxxx# cd
root@xxxxxxx# cd /tensorflow
root@xxxxxxx:/tensorflow# git pull
```

Step 6: Retrain Inception
It's now time to re-train Inception with our images! We will do this by launching the Python file *retrain.py* and defining a number of its parameters. Depending on your dataset size, training might take 5 minutes or 45, or even longer. If you are training two categories using 60-100 images per category, this should only take ~10 minutes on a modern PC or Mac. Note that you may have issues or errors if you use very small data sets, e.g., 10 or 15 images. It is recommended that you use at minimum 20 images per category.

While still in the Docker container, type the following. Make sure to type everything, including the "--" and "\". If you are not in the container for some reason, re-type docker - run -it.... from Step 4.

```
root@xxxxxxx:/tensorflow# cd
root@xxxxxxx# python
tensorflow/examples/image_retraining/retrain.py \
--bottleneck_dir=/tf_files/bottlenecks \
--how_many_training_steps 500 \
--model_dir=/tf_files/inception \
--output_graph=/tf_files/retrained_graph.pb \
--output_labels=/tf_files/retrained_labels.txt \
--image_dir /tf_files/reptiles
```

Note: the directory on Line 2 must be accurate. If it is not, you will be told that retrain.py does not exist. In some cases, the directory might be buried within an extra tensorflow directory, such as below:

```
/tensorflow/tensorflow/examples/images_retraining/retrain.p
y
```

This will train for a while. You will see a long list that looks like the following:

```
Creating bottleneck at
/tf_files/bottlenecks/snake/anaconda.jpg.txt
Creating bottleneck at
/tf_files/bottlenecks/lizard/chameleon.jpg.txt
2017-03-09 22:46:19.250688: Step 0: Train accuracy = 45.0%
2017-03-09 22:46:19.250819: Step 0: Cross entropy =
1.528518
2017-03-09 22:46:23.379481: Step 0: Validation accuracy =
37.0% (N=100)
```

Once it is complete, you will see a final accuracy printout.

```
Final test accuracy = 87.3% (N=387)
Converted 2 variables to const ops.
```

Step 7: Download Python Gist

Our last step before classifying is to download a Python file called *label_image.py* that is stored in a Github *gist*. On a high level, this file enables us to input an image, say of a *lizard*, and then have Inception predict its class. It is built using Python and Tensorflow.

To do this, exit Docker by pressing:

```
root@xxxxxxx# ctrl-d
```

Then, use the *curl* command to download the *gist* file to the *tf_file* directory.

```
~$ curl -L https://goo.gl/tx3dqg >
$HOME/tf_files/label_image.py
```

Step 8: Classify

Now we can classify! To do this, we must restart our Docker container with our Tensorflow image and files. Type:

```
~$ docker run -it -v $HOME/tf_files:/tf_files
gcr.io/tensorflow/tensorflow:latest-devel
```

Then, all we need to do is launch the *label_image.py* Python file and include an image that we want Inception to classify. This line is long!

```
root@xxxxxxx# python /tf_files/label_image.py
/tf_files/reptiles/snake/viper.jpg
```

You will then see the following. This is what we have been waiting for!

```
Snake (score = 0.9431)
Lizard (score = 0.2156)
```

And as you can see, Inception has predicted at ~94% that our *viper* image is a snake, which is fantastic!

Next Steps:

If you want to experiment and take this further, here are a few ideas to get you started:

Classifying Different Images

To classify any type of image, simply alter the folders and images in Step 3! That's it. The rest of the steps remain the exact same. If you are wondering where you can find image datasets, here are some fantastic options:

- UCI Machine Learning Repository
- YouTube 8M Dataset
- Deep Learning Dataset List

Modifying The Parameters

Modify/add to the parameters we defined in Step 6. From increasing or decreasing training steps to altering the testing batch size, there are many to choose from. These include:

[--image_dir IMAGE_DIR] [--output_graph OUTPUT_GRAPH]

```
[--summaries_dir SUMMARIES_DIR]
[--learning_rate LEARNING_RATE]
[--testing_percentage TESTING_PERCENTAGE]
[--validation_percentage VALIDATION_PERCENTAGE]
[--eval_step_interval EVAL_STEP_INTERVAL]
[--train_batch_size TRAIN_BATCH_SIZE]
[--test_batch_size TEST_BATCH_SIZE]
[--validation_batch_size VALIDATION_BATCH_SIZE]
[--print_misclassified_test_images] [--model_dir MODEL_DIR]
[--final_tensor_name FINAL_TENSOR_NAME] [--flip_left_right]
[--random_crop RANDOM_CROP] [--random_scale RANDOM_SCALE]
  [--random_brightness RANDOM_BRIGHTNESS]
```

Learn More With Google's Codelab

3. Read the Google Codelabs "Tensorflow for Poets" tutorial. This tutorial covers exactly what we have done here, but adds a few layers of detail.

Part 4

A Brief History of
Neural Networks

Ch. 30

A Brief History of Neural Networks

It all began in 1943.

In 1943, neurophysiologist Warren McCulloch and mathematician Walter Pitts published a paper on how neurons in the brain might function. This publication was one of the initial works that sparked an interest and fascination with both neural networks and artificial intelligence. Along with the paper, the pair also constructed a basic electrical circuit to demonstrate their theory.

In 1949, Donald Hebb expanded on the idea presented by McCulloch and Pitts by proposing that neural pathways actually *strengthened* with each use. This theory was published in Hebb's book *The Organization of Behavior,* and is technically known as *Hebbian Learning* (often summed up as *"Cells that fire together, wire together".*)

During the 1950's computer technology began to advance, and it was during this time that the theories presented in the previous decade could be put to test. An IBM researcher named Nathaniel Rochester led the first effort at constructing an artificial neural network, but failed. Later attempts were successful however, and in 1954 the first Hebbian network was implemented at MIT.

For a variety of reasons interest in the field of neural networks dipped from the 1960's into the early 1980's. It wasn't until the rise of personal computing power and availability of large scale data that interests began to shift again in the mid 1980's. For the next few decades a series of papers, events and the development of computer technology helped push forward the idea of artificial intelligence and importance of neural networks.

Major events/papers include:

- **1956: A boom in interest and funding.** In 1956 the Dartmouth Summer Research Project on Artificial Intelligence was held at Dartmouth College in Hanover, New Hampshire. The conference was the product of four men from Dartmouth, Harvard, IBM, and Bell, who had a year earlier proposed that a 2 month, 10 man study of artificial intelligence take place. One of the main areas of interest was neural networks.

The result of this research project was an increased interest in AI and neural processing.

- **1958: The development of the perceptron.** The idea of the perceptron was first proposed in 1958 by Frank Roenblatt, a psychologist at Cornell. He proposed the idea of the *Mark 1 Perceptron,* a simple input-output system modeled on McCulloch and Pitts proposal a decade earlier. The *Mark 1 Perceptron* consisted of the following:

  The only downfall was that it could only solve linear problems (AND, OR). Non-linear problems using (XOR) could not be solved.

- **1959: Solving a real-world application.** The first neural network applied to a real world problem was developed in 1959 by Stanford researchers Bernard Widrow and Marcian (Ted) Hoff. Named MADALINE, the neural network made use of an adaptive filter that eliminated the echo on phone lines. Widrow is still a professor at Stanford.

- **1982: The development of the Hopfield Net.** In 1982 Jon Hopfield of Caltech presented a paper to the National Academy of Sciences that demonstrated what neural networks could and *could not* achieve. He also popularized a form of a recurrent neural network (RNN) which came to be known as a *Hopfield net.*

Now, in 2017 and beyond, the race to build artificial intelligence is continuing to intensify.With technology continuing to progress alongside computing power, it is becoming easier for individuals and companies alike to delve into AI and its sub-fields, such as neural networks.

As of early 2017, AI is currently used by many tech giants including Microsoft, Apple, Uber, Google,Facebook, and IBM.

Part 5

Additional Resources

Ch. 31

Extended Definitions for Neural Networks

Welcome to our expanded definitions section. In this section we aim to cover core definitions of terms that are often used in neural networks, and have done our best to explain each term in easy to understand language. We have also provided links for further research and examples where appropriate.

Please note that this list is not exhaustive and that all definitions are within the broader context of machine learning and neural networks specifically.

We have organized this section into the following:

1. Terms that are often confusing but describe the same function, action or object. For example, edge and synapse or node and neuron.
2. General definitions associated with neural networks.

Terms That Describe the Same Function, Action or Object

Activation function or transfer function? Node or neuron? Synapse or edge or connection? Which is correct - or are any acceptable? If you have dipped your toes in the world of machine learning, you'll have quickly realized that there is a lack of consistency when it comes to basic terminology used.

To help bring clarity to this, we have put together a list of common terms that are often used interchangeably to refer to the same function, action or object. **Again, please note that all terms are defined within the context of machine learning and neural networks specifically**.

Terms

Activation Function vs Transfer Function = These are the same
*For this guide we have opted to use the term activation function.

Definition: An activation function defines the output of a node given a set of inputs. There are many types of activation functions. The two most common types of activation functions used in neural networks are the Logistic (also called Sigmoid) and Hyperbolic Tangent. Why is this ?

There are two reasons:

1. First, they introduce nonlinearity to a neural network. This is critical because most problems that a NN solves are nonlinear, i.e., they cannot be solved by separating classes with a straight line. The other activation functions in the chart above, such as Step, Sign and Linear, do not introduce nonlinearity.

   2. Second, they limit the output of a node to a certain range. The logistic function produces output between 0 to 1. The Hyperbolic Tangent produces output between -1 to 1.

Also note that Transfer function is sometimes used to denote other aspects of a neural network. See its own definition further down this list for details.

Artificial Neural Network vs Neural Network = These are the same
*For this guide we have opted to use the term neural network.

Definition: Neural Networks (NN) are one type of learning algorithm that is used within machine learning. They are modeled on the human brain and nervous system and the goal of NN's is to process information in a similar way to the human brain. NN's are composed of a large number of highly interconnected processing elements (nodes) working in parallel to solve a specific problem. A key feature of a NN is that it learns by example.

Node vs Neuron = These are the same
*For this guide we have opted to use the term node.

Definition: Inside of an artificial neural network, nodes represent the neurons within a human brain. A neural network consists of multiple layers (input, hidden, and output), and each of these layers consists of either one or multiple nodes. These nodes are all connected and work together to solve a problem.

Synapse vs Edge vs Connection = These are the same
*For this guide we have opted to use the term edge.

Definition: A neural network consists of multiple layers (input, hidden, and output), and each of these layers consists of either one or multiple nodes. These nodes are all connected via edges, which mimic the synapse connections found within the human brain.

Target vs Desired Output Value vs Target Variable vs Ideal Output = These are the same
*For this guide we have opted to use the term target.

Definition: Neural networks are supervised learning algorithms, which means that the network is provided with a training set. This training set provides targets that the network aims to achieve. Technically speaking, the target is the desired output for the given input.

Target is usually denoted as "T" and the input denoted as "X".

Total Error Vs Global Error = These are the same
*For this guide we have opted to use the term total error.

A neural network is successfully trained once it has minimized (to an acceptable level) the difference between its *real* or *actual* output and its *target* output. This difference that the network strives to minimize is technically called an *error* or *total error*.

Additional details: The *total error* is the sum of all *local errors*. A *local error* is the difference that occurs between the *actual* output of a single node and the *target* output that was expected. For example:

>Actual output: 0.75
>Target output: 1.0
>Error: 0.25

If a network has multiple output nodes, the *final local error* is the sum of error of all output nodes, i.e., all *local errors*.

The *total error* is typically calculated using a cost function such as mean square error (MSE) or root mean square (RMS).

Total Net Input Vs Net Input = These are the same
*For this guide we have opted to use the term net input.

Definition: Total input refers to the sum of all inputs into a hidden or output node. It is calculated by adding together the multiplication of each input by its respective weight. This calculation is usually performed using the summation operator. See below.

General Definitions
A short concise definition is first provided for each term, followed by additional details that dive into the nitty-gritty.

Algorithm
An algorithm is a set of instructions designed to perform a specific task.

Additional Details: First and foremost, a NN is an algorithm. More precisely, it is a specific type of machine learning algorithm (along with other algorithms such as random forests, decision trees, nearest neighbors, and many others). Apart from this, algorithms are used *within a NN to* successfully train the network. One of the most common algorithms used to accomplish this task is backpropagation, which makes use of gradient descent to optimize and ultimately train the network.

Artificial Intelligence
Artificial Intelligence (AI) is an area within computer science that aims to develop machines capable of imitating intelligent human behavior.

Additional Details: Neural networks are part of what is called Deep Learning, which is a branch of machine learning. The goal of Deep Learning is to move machine learning towards artificial intelligence. Machine learning is the science of getting computers to act without being explicitly programmed.

Batch Training
Batch training (also called "Full Batch") is a particular form of gradient descent, which is used in conjunction with back propagation to train a network. Stochastic (also called online) and mini-batch training are other popular forms of gradient descent. Each method has its own strengths and shortcomings.

Additional Details: Batch training works by summing the gradients for each training set element and then updating the weights. This updating is technically one iteration. In contrast, online training also updates the weights, but it does so for every training set element - not their sums. This means that online training incorporates many more iterations than batch training.

Chain Rule
The chain rule can be hard to understand. Here are two definitions:

- The chain rule is a way to find a derivative of an equation that is a function found inside another function.

- The chain rule is used to compute the derivative of the composition of two or more functions.

Additional Details: Within a neural network, the chain rule is used to calculate the derivative across an entire neural network. Practically speaking, this makes it possible to adjust the weights and (hopefully) succeed in training the network.

Classification

Classification refers to the sorting, or classifying, of data into groups. For example, a neural network might be presented with a folder of various pictures: some are dogs, others are cats, and others are birds. In this instance, the job of the neural network is to learn how to classify these pictures into three respective groups: dogs, cats, and birds.

Additional Details: Neural networks excel at classification. A fantastic example is Google's Photos app, which is able to organize your photos for you even if you haven't manually tagged them.

Convolutional Neural Network (CNN or ConvNet)

A convolutional neural network (CNN) is a specific type of feedforward neural network. CNN's are typically used with image recognition and in many regards are the core of computer vision systems. However, they are also used in natural language processing.

At a basic level, CNN's have an architecture that is inspired by the animal visual cortex. This architecture naturally lends itself to top-notch performance with image recognition.

Converge

Within machine learning, *converging* refers to the output moving closer and closer to the desired target value. For example, if the desired target value is "1", and the output continually inches closer to 1, it is converging, and if the output were to become "1", it would *converge*.

The opposite of converge is to diverge, which occurs when the output continues to oscillate (undergo fluctuations). In this circumstance, the output is not inching steadily towards the target value, but is fluctuating instead.

Curse of Dimensionality

The curse of dimensionality is a machine learning phrase that refers to the difficulty of working in multiple dimensions.

Additional details: A dimension is an attribute - or several attributes - that describe a property. With neural networks dimensions are the *inputs* to the network.

For example, if an image is broken into pixels and the result fed into a neural network, the number of inputs will equal the number of individual pixels. For a 32x32 image, this would equate to 1,024 inputs - or dimensions.

Herein is where the problem lies: The goal of training a neural network is to find the best combination of weights that yields the lowest error rate - but, the more dimensions that exist, the greater the amount of weight adjustments and combinations *also exist.* With current computing power, the ability to compute *every single combination* soon becomes impossible, even in low-dimensional networks. This problem is what the curse of dimensionality refers to.

To overcome this problem, workarounds - or shortcuts - such as gradient descent are often used.

Dropout

Dropout is a form of regularization that helps a network *generalize* its fittings and increase accuracy. It is often used with deep neural networks to combat overfitting, which it accomplishes by occasionally *switching off* one or more nodes in the network.

A node that is switched off cannot have its weights updated, nor can it affect other nodes. This causes the other weights that are switched on to become *more insensitive* to the weights of other nodes and, eventually, begin to make better decisions on their own.

Deep Learning

Deep Learning is a relatively new field within machine learning that refers to neural networks with multiple hidden layers. The adjective "deep" refers to the amount of hidden layers that exist; the more layers, the "deeper" the learning. The goal of deep learning is to enable machine learning to achieve its goal of creating artificial intelligence.

Epoch

An epoch refers to one forward pass and one backward pass of *all training examples* in a neural network. For example, if you are training a network to recognize images and have a set of 10,000 images, these images are the training examples. An epoch will have occurred once all of the examples are passed through the network. "Passing through the network" includes both a forward and backward pass through the network.

In other words, an epoch describes the number of times a network sees an *entire data set*.

Additional details: Other terms often confused with epoch include batch and iteration.

A *batch* refers to the total number of training examples in both a forward *and* backward pass. For example, 100 images.

An *iteration* refers to the number of times a "batch" of data passes through the network.

Here is an example using all three terms: If you have 500 images (training examples), and your batch size is 100, then it will take 5 iterations to complete 1 epoch.

Gradient

A gradient is the slope of the error function at a specific weight - or in other words, it is the individual error of a single weight in a neural network. Technically it is a vector and arrived at by calculating the derivative of the slope at a specific point.

Additional details: Optimization methods such as gradient descent (see below), calculate the gradients (or errors) of each weight with the aim of minimizing those errors each time they are calculated. This minimization can be viewed as moving down a hill, or descending - and the farther down the hill you go, the less the error is. The ultimate goal is to reduce the *global error* (which is the sum of all local errors) to as minimal as possible.

Gradient Descent

Gradient descent is a popular *optimization* method used to train neural networks, and is commonly used in conjunction with *backpropagation*. *Optimization* refers to minimizing the total error (often called global error) of the network to an acceptable level. The *total error* is often calculated using a method such as Mean Square Error (MSE) or Root Mean Square (RMS).

Hyperparameter

Within machine learning, the term hyperparameter refers to the "knobs" that one can adjust to minimize errors and train a network. Unlike other parameters in a neural network, hyperparameters cannot be learned by the network. In light of this, hyperparameters must be assigned and adjusted manually.

Examples of hyperparameters include:
- Total number of input nodes
- Total number of hidden layers
- Total number of hidden nodes
- Total number of output nodes
- Weight values
- Bias values
- Learning Rate

Additional optional hyperparameters include:
- Learning rate schedule (learning rate decay)
- Momentum (optional)
- Mini-batch size
- Number of training iterations
- Weight decay

Examples of standard model parameters that a network can learn include:
- Weights
- Biases

Learning Rate Schedule

A learning rate schedule allows for the learning rate to be adjusted (usually decreased) while a network is training.

Local Minima

A *local minima* is a false *global minimum.* In other words, it is a false minimal error that neural networks tend to become trapped in and unable to escape. *Momentum* is a popular technique used to help push a network out of it and towards a true *global minimum,* or at least in order to find a local minima that is closer to the true minimum and thus acceptable.

Machine Learning

Machine learning (often abbreviated as ML), is both a field within computer science and also a type of artificial intelligence. At its most basic level, the goal of ML is to create computers that can act *without* being programmed. ML makes use of algorithms to parse (break apart and analyze) data, learn from that data, and then act on that data.

Overfitting

Overfitting occurs when a network performs well with a *specific training set* and minimizes the error, but when presented with a *new* training set the error rate is much larger. For example, say that a neural network successfully trains (minimizes the error) on a data set containing three types of animals: cats, dogs, dogs and birds. However, when a *new* training set of cats, dogs, and birds is introduced to the network, the error is significantly larger.

This often occurs because the network only *appears* to have successfully learned, but in reality has merely "memorized" the initial training set.

On a more technical level, overfitting occurs when a network pays too much attention to unnecessary details called *noise* instead of paying attention to the *signal.*

Parameter

There are two types of parameters within machine learning: model parameters and hyperparameters.

Model parameters can be adjusted by the network itself. In fact, this adjustment is what constitutes the "learning" of a network. Example model parameters include the weights.

Hyperparameter refers to the "knobs" that one can adjust to minimize errors and train a network. Unlike other parameters in a neural network, hyperparameters cannot be learned by the network. In light of this, hyperparameters must be assigned and adjusted manually. Examples include momentum and the learning rate.

Propagation

There are two types of propagation within a neural network: forward propagation and backpropagation. Forward propagation refers to moving data through the network to get output. This output is then compared with the *target* output and any difference is labelled as an error (also called *global error*).

Backpropagation refers to moving *back through the network* and updating the weights. An *optimization* method such as *gradient descent* is often used to do this.

Recurrent Neural Network (RNN)

A recurrent neural network (RNN) is specific type of neural network that contains at least *one feedback connection* - or in other words, a loop. RNN's have shown great promise at learning sequences and performing sequence recognition and association. Applications have included language processing and speech recognition.

There are number of RNN models (architectures), including :
- Fully recurrent network
- Recursive neural network
- Hopfield network

Regularization

Within machine learning, regularization refers to various techniques that are used to prevent overfitting. Penalizing the cost function is a popular technique.

Semi-Supervised Learning

Semi-Supervised learning is one of three types of categories used in machine learning. It is a blend of supervised and unsupervised learning.

Stochastic Gradient Descent (SGD)

Stochastic Gradient Descent (sometimes abbreviated as SGD and/or called *online training or online gradient descent*) is* one of three popular *gradient descent* variants. It is used to optimize a neural network by minimizing the error (also called *global error*). The other popular gradient descent variants are *batch training* and *mini-batch training*.

Additional details: With SGD, the weights in a network are modified after every training set example. What this means is that a *single* training set example is used to update a parameter (weight) in a particular iteration. If a training set is large and has many examples, this can take a long time.

*SGD is technically one type of online training algorithm, but we won't go into the details here. On a high-level, many in the ML field use the terms SGD and *online training* interchangeably.

Supervised Learning

Supervised learning is one of three types of models used in machine learning. In fact, supervised learning algorithms such as neural networks and support vector machines are typically what people think of as artificial intelligence and machine learning.

With supervised learning, the data is a set of training examples with the associated "correct answers". The algorithm learns to predict the correct answer from this training set. An example of this would be learning to predict whether an email is spam if given a million emails, each of which is labeled as "spam" or "not spam".

Classification and regression are two examples of problems often solved using supervised learning.

Additional details: Technically, with supervised learning there is an input (typically denoted as X) and output (often denoted as Y), and an algorithm is used to map the functions from input to output. The input (x) is the training example, the output (Y) is the correct answer, and the algorithm can be any machine learning model, such as a neural network, support vector machine (SVM) or random forest.

Training Set

A training set (also called training data) consists of a set of *training examples*. For example, if you were training a network to analyze handwritten numbers between 1-10, a training example would be a single handwritten digit, such as 9. The training set would be all of the handwritten digits together.

In supervised learning, each *training example* is a pair that consists of an input and output (the "correct answer" of what the input is). The goal of supervised learning is to correctly *map* the input data to the output data, and thus *learn*.

Transfer Function

The term *transfer function* is often applied to different aspects of a neural network. This can make the term incredibly confusing. For sake of clarity, we have opted to not use this term in our book. Possible uses include:

- Referring to the activation function. This is the most common usage for this term, although activation function is the more popular of the pair.
- Referring to the summation function.
- Referring to the summation function and activation function combined.

Unsupervised Learning

Unsupervised learning is one of three types of models used in machine learning. With this type of learning, an algorithm is provided with an input (typically denoted as X), *but no target output* (typically denoted as Y).

Since an unsupervised algorithm does not have any "correct answer" variables (Y) to learn from, it instead tries to find trends in the data. This of course is the exact opposite of how supervised learning works (which is provided with both an input X and target output Y).

Examples of unsupervised learning algorithms involve clustering (grouping similar data points) and anomaly detection (detecting unusual data points in a data set).

Vector

A vector represents a quantity that has two attributes: magnitude (size) and direction. Vectors can be summed and subtracted from one another, and to perform a calculation, vectors are typically broken up in **x** and **y** parts.

Within a neural network, a vector is basically a special type of matrix that has only one column. A vector is an n x 1 matrix, where n represents the number of rows, and 1 represents a single column. Vectors *always* have 1 column in a neural network, and are sometimes referred to as having n-dimensions.

Text Editors and Python Libraries

Popular Python Libraries

Libraries are an incredible tool that can speed up the coding process and help create more robust and powerful programs. Python itself has a fantastic and extensive library that includes many built-in functions such as *len*, and modules such as *datetime* and *csv*. These functions and modules come in very handy when coding popular tasks and help make your life *a lot easier*.

On top of this, there are also many other libraries built specifically for Python and machine learning in particular. And the best part? Most, if not all, are free to use and easy to access.

All-Purpose Libraries

Some of the most popular general purpose libraries for Python are listed below. All descriptions are taken from each respective libraries website. Unless noted, all libraries are free to use.

Note: You will see **PIP Installation** below. PIP is a package management system that is used to install programs written in Python. It comes pre-installed with Python 2.7.9+ and Python 3.4+, and works on Unix/Linux, macOS and Windows.

If a library has provided separate installation instructions for Windows, we also provide a link to that.

BeautifulSoup

Mmmm. Beautifulsoup. If you are wanting to scrap a website, Beautifulsoup is the library for you. It is fantastic at pulling data out of HTML and XML files. Examples include pulling text, links, and URL's.

Python Compatibility: Python 2 and 3 are supported.
PIP Installation: `pip install beautifulsoup4`
Official Website: https://www.crummy.com/software/BeautifulSoup/

Matplotlib

Pie charts ? Histograms ? Bar charts ? Matplotlib is *the* 2D plotting library for Python, and likely one of languages most popular libraries.

Python Compatibility: Python 2 and 3 are supported.
PIP Installation:

```
python -m pip install -U pip setuptools
python -m pip install matplotlib
```

Official Website: http://matplotlib.org/

NLTK

NLTK is the "leading platform for building Python programs to work with human language data". Over 50 lexicons and corpora resources are available through NLTK. Seriously - it's a goldmine for anything language focused.

Python Compatibility: Python 2 and 3 are supported.
PIP Installation (Mac): `sudo pip install -U nltk`
Installation (Windows): http://www.nltk.org/install.html.
Official Website: http://www.nltk.org/

Numpy

Numpy is incredible at creating robust and powerful arrays. It also has great broadcasting functions and is useful for linear algebra and random number capabilities. It many regards, it is the go-to library for scientific computing.

Python Compatibility: Python 2 and 3 are supported.
Installation: http://www.scipy.org/scipylib/download.html.
Official Website: http://www.numpy.org/

Requests

The NSA. Twitter. Google. Paypal. Her Majesty's Government. Amazon. According to Request's official website, the above organizations and institutions "claim to use Requests internally". What does requests do exactly? It is a library that allows you to send HTTP/1.1 requests.

Python Compatibility: Python 2 and 3 are supported.
PIP Installation: `pip install requests`
Official Website: http://docs.python-requests.org/en/master/

Scipy

Scipy is a very popular eco-system of libraries for Python - basically a one-stop-shop for anything mathematics, science, and engineering focused. Some of the top-notch libraries include Numpy, Scipy, Matplotlib, pandas, Sympy. IPython (Jupyter) is also included.

Python Compatibility: Python 2 and 3 are supported.
PIP Installation (Mac):
`pip install --user numpy scipy matplotlib ipython jupyter pandas sympy nose`
Installation (Windows): http://www.scipy.org/install.html.
Official Website: http://www.scipy.org/

Scrapy

If you are looking to create a spider for scraping websites, Scrapy is an excellent choice. Scrapy is a framework that allows you to extract data from websites - and it is fast.

Python Compatibility: Python 2 and 3 are supported.
PIP Installation: `pip install scrapy`
Official Website: https://scrapy.org/

Machine Learning Libraries

Some of the most popular libraries can be found below. Most are open source and actively developed by the machine learning community. There are lots of links included, so be sure to dig deeper into a library that interests you.

Note: You will see the terms **library** and **framework** used below. Many authors and programmers disagree on the exact difference between the two. Here is a simplified definition for each.

A library is a collection of code related to a specific task (or closely related tasks). With a library, you *call it* and you are in control.

A framework is a collection of libraries and can be viewed as an environment to build on. With a framework you are not in control. The framework *calls you*.

Or, to put it another way: if a library is a toolbox, a framework is the shop. A framework is a step-up from a toolbox.

Caffe

Caffe is deep learning framework designed for working with images. It is powerful, fast, and quite popular. Caffe was developed by Yangqing Jia while he completed his Ph.D. at UC Berkeley. Jia currently works as a research scientist at Facebook, and previously worked on the Tensoflow project Google Brain.

Caffe highlights:

- *Image processing*. Caffe is a machine-vision library.
- *Speed*. It can process over 60 million images per day.
- *CNN's*. Caffe performs images classification using convolutional neural networks.

Installation: Caffe can be installed via Docker, Ubuntu, OS X, Fedora, Windows, OpenCL and AWS. See http://caffe.berkeleyvision.org/installation.html.

Official Website: http://caffe.berkeleyvision.org/

Keras

Keras is a high-level neural network that works *on top of* Tensorflow or Theano. In a nutshell, it makes creating and running a neural network much easier and faster by *minimizing* complexity and *cutting down* on coding required. Keras was developed (and is maintained) by Francois Chollet, a Google engineer. According to Chollet's LinkedIn profile, Keras is used at companies such as Netflix, Square, Yelp and Google.

Keras highlights:

- Fast prototyping.
- Supports CNN's and RNN's.
- Runs on both CPU and GPU.

Installation: https://keras.io/#installation.

Pandas

If you need to work with structured data or time series data, pandas is a great library to use. Pandas makes data analysis and modelling much easier in Python. On a side note, Pandas is technically spelled all lowercase (pandas). Pandas is used in many sectors, including Finance, Economics, and Web Analytics.

Pandas highlights:

- Reshaping of data sets.
- Powerful aggregating and transforming of data.
- Very fast data manipulation.

Installation: Pandas recommends installation via Anaconda. For official documentation, http://pandas.pydata.org/pandas-docs/stable/install.html.
Official Website: http://pandas.pydata.org/

PyBrain

PyBrain is a machine learning library that is no longer actively developed, but it is still a great library - especially for individuals who are new to ML. In fact, PyBrain was developed for students new to the field of machine learning and is not technically high-level (like Keras), but is up there!

PyBrain highlights:

- Designed for individuals new to machine learning.
- Plenty of documentation.

Installation: http://pybrain.org/docs/#installation.
Official Website: http://pybrain.org/

Scikit-learn

Scikit-learn is a machine learning library that makes data mining a much easier and faster task. Scikit-learn is built on Numpy, Scipy and

Matplotlib. It is excellent at classification, regression, clustering, preprocessing, model selection, and dimensionality reduction.

Scikit-learn highlights:

- Great for classification, e.g., spam classification, image recognition.
- Plenty of tutorials.

Installation: http://scikit-learn.org/stable/install.html.
Official Website: http://scikit-learn.org/stable/

Tensorflow

Tensorflow is an open source machine learning library developed by Google. It supports deep learning (neural nets with multiple hidden layers) as well as reinforcement learning. Tensorflow is used in Google's speech recognition systems, Google Photo's, Gmail, and search. It is quite new (2015), but is rapidly gaining popularity within the ML field.

Tensorflow highlights:
- Runs on both CPU and GPU.
- Very powerful and continually being developed.
- Many official tutorials

Installation:
https://www.tensorflow.org/versions/r0.12/get_started/os_setup.html#download-and-setup.
Official Website: https://www.tensorflow.org/

Theano

Released in 2008, Theano is a deep learning library that does a fantastic job handling arrays and exploring data. Theano allows users to define, optimize and evaluate mathematical expressions.

Theano highlights:

- Great at problem-solving large amounts of data.
- Very fast (compared to using Python and Numpy alone).
- Top-notch official tutorials.

Installation: http://deeplearning.net/software/theano/install.html.
Official Website: http://deeplearning.net/software/theano/

Popular Text Editors

Atom

Atom is a self-described "hackable text editor for the 21st Century". It is built by the folks at Github and offers the following features:

- *Platforms:* Atom works on multiple platforms, including OS X, Windows and Linux.
- *Packages:* Packages can be installed directly from within Atom.
- *Autocompletion:* An autocomplete function speeds up coding - and with less errors.

Cost: Free
Platforms: OS X, Windows 7 or later, and Linux.
Official Website: https://atom.io/

BBEdit

BBEdit is a professional HTML and text editor. It is developed by the Bare Bones Software team and is continually being updated.

Features include:

- *Grep:* Grep pattern matching is built-in.
- *Coloring:* Syntax coloring is offered for numerous languages.
- *Markup:* A complete set of HTML markup tools are built-in.

Cost: $49.99 USD
Platforms: OS X only.
Official Website:
http://www.barebones.com/products/bbedit/index.html

Brackets

Brackets is an open source and lightweight text editor that incorporates visual tools into the editor itself. It was founded by Adobe and is specifically designed to meet the needs of web designers and front-end developers.

Features include:

- *Inline Editing:* Code can be edited within a file via a window - which means there is no need to jump to another tab.

- *Extensions:* Many extensions exist, including Git integration and W3C Validation.
- *Videos:* A variety of excellent training videos are offered on brackets.io

Cost: Free
Platforms: OS X, Windows and Linux
Official Website: http://brackets.io/

Emacs
GNU Emacs is an open source text editor that is highly customizable and powerful.

Features include:
- *Coloring:* Syntax coloring for many different file types.
- *Package System:* A package system is built-in for downloading and installing extensions.
- *Documentation:* fantastic tutorials are offered on the official GNU Emacs website.

Cost: Free
Platforms: OS X, Windows and Linux. Other platforms including GNU and FreeBSD are also compatible.
Official Website: https://www.gnu.org/software/emacs/

Jupyter (formally IPython)
Jupyter is a notebook that operates as a web application and allows for documents (including live code) to be created and shared. One of the major strengths of Jupyter is that, like an IDE, code can be run within the notebook. Jupyter is very popular and currently used by major corporations such as Google, Microsoft, IBM, and Bloomberg.

Features include:
- *Explanatory Text:* Text that explains what is happening on a certain line of code can be added. This makes sharing, understanding and debugging much easier.
- *Language Support:* Over 40 languages are supported, including Python, R, and Scala.
- *Sharing:* Notebooks can be shared via email, Dropbox, GitHub - and of course via Juypter itself.

Cost: Free
Platforms: OS X, Windows and Linux.
Official Website: http://jupyter.org/

Sublime Text

Sublime Text is a cross platform text editor that is incredibly popular amongst Python enthusiasts. New versions (builds) of the program are constantly being released.

Features include:
- *Split Editing:* Files can be edited side-by-side, or two locations can be edited in the same file.
- *Customization*: Menus, snippets, macros - almost anything in Sublime is customizable.
- *Distraction Free Mode:* Sublime offers a full screen editing mode that minimizes distractions.

Cost: $70.00 USD
Platforms: OS X, Windows and Linux.
Official Website: https://www.sublimetext.com/

Platforms: Anaconda

Anaconda is an open data science platform that is incredibly robust and offers a wide variety of useful features. The platform is data science focused, which means it is rich resource for data scientists and others. Anaconda is currently used by millions around the world, and is constantly being developed and tweaked.

The basic version of the platform is free.

Features include:

- The ability to run multiple versions of Python in separate, isolated environments.
- Pre-bundling of 100 of the most popular Python, R and Scale packages. Python packages include Numpy, Pandas, and Matplotlib - among many others.
- Easy access and installation of 720 more packages.
- A number of IDE's such as Jupyter and Spyder.
- Integration with Sublime Text2 and PyCharm.
- A graphical interface installer or command line installer.

Anaconda can be downloaded for Windows, OS X and Linux.

Bibliography

Albright, Dan. "Text Editors vs. IDEs: Which One Is Better For
Programmers?" *MakeUseOf*. N.p., 23 Nov. 2015. Web. 08 Dec.
2016. <http://www.makeuseof.com/tag/text-editors-vs-ides-one-
better-programmers/>.

"Artificial Neural Network." *Wikipedia*. Wikimedia Foundation, n.d. Web.
08 Dec. 2016.
<https://en.wikipedia.org/wiki/Artificial_neural_network>.

"Artificial Neural Networks Technology." University of Toronto, n.d.
Web. 08 Dec. 2016.
<http://www.psych.utoronto.ca/users/reingold/courses/ai/cache/neur
al_ToC.html>.

Bengio, Yoshua. "Practical Recommendations for Gradient-Based
Training of Deep Architectures." *Lecture Notes in Computer Science
Neural Networks: Tricks of the Trade* (2012): 437-78. 16 Sept. 2012.
Web. 5 Jan. 2017.

Bradford, Laurence. "Learn About Text Editors In Five Minutes Or Less."
Learn to Code With Me. N.p., 08 May 2015. Web. 08 Dec. 2016.
<http://learntocodewith.me/programming/basics/text-editors/>.

Britz, Denny. "Deep Learning Glossary." *WildML*. N.p., 28 Jan. 2016.
Web. 08 Dec. 2016. <http://www.wildml.com/deep-learning-
glossary/>.

Brownlee, Jason. "A Tour of Machine Learning Algorithms." *Machine
Learning Mastery*. N.p., 15 Nov. 2016. Web. 9 Dec. 2016.
<http://machinelearningmastery.com/a-tour-of-machine-learning-
algorithms/>.

Bullinaria, John. "Recurrent Neural Networks." *Artificial Neural
Networks* (n.d.): 61-69. 2015. Web. 13 Dec. 2016.

Burch, Carl. "Floating-point Representation." *Toves*. N.p., Sept. 2011.
Web. 03 Mar. 2017. <http://www.toves.org/books/float/>.

"Caffe." *Caffe | Deep Learning Framework*. N.p., n.d. Web. 12 Dec. 2016.
<http://caffe.berkeleyvision.org/>.

Christensson, Per. "The Tech Terms Computer Dictionary." *The Tech
Terms Computer Dictionary*. N.p., n.d. Web. 08 Dec. 2016.
<http://techterms.com/>.

Clabaugh, Caroline, Dave Myszewski, and Jimmy Pang. "Neural

Networks - History." *Neural Networks - History*. Stanford
University, n.d. Web. 08 Dec. 2016.
<http://cs.stanford.edu/people/eroberts/courses/soco/projects/neural-networks/History/history1.html>.

"Convolutional Neural Network." *Wikipedia*. Wikimedia Foundation, n.d.
Web. 09 Dec. 2016.
<https://en.wikipedia.org/wiki/Convolutional_neural_network>.

"CS231n Convolutional Neural Networks for Visual Recognition."
CS231n Convolutional Neural Networks for Visual Recognition.
N.p., n.d. Web. 09 Dec. 2016. <http://cs231n.github.io/neural-networks-1/>.

Dean, Lon. "Artificial Neural Networks Technology." *History of Neural
Networks*. N.p., n.d. Web. 14 Dec. 2016.
<http://www.psych.utoronto.ca/users/reingold/courses/ai/cache/neural4.html>.

Gallagher, Daniel. "Cost Functions in a Neural Network." *Machine
Philosopher*. N.p., 27 Nov. 2016. Web. 19 Dec. 2016.
<http://www.machinephilosopher.com/cost-function-neural-network-intro/>.

Gibson, Chris Nicholson Adam. "DL4J vs. Torch vs. Theano vs. Caffe vs.
TensorFlow." *Deep Learning Comp Sheet: Deeplearning4j vs. Torch
vs. Theano vs. Caffe vs. TensorFlow vs. MxNet vs. CNTK -
Deeplearning4j: Open-source, Distributed Deep Learning for the
JVM*. Skymind, n.d. Web. 12 Dec. 2016.
<https://deeplearning4j.org/compare-dl4j-torch7-pylearn>.

Gorner, Martin. "TensorFlow and Deep Learning, without a PhD."
TensorFlow and Deep Learning, without a PhD. N.p., 6 Feb. 2017.
Web. 03 Mar. 2017.
<https://codelabs.developers.google.com/codelabs/cloud-tensorflow-mnist/index.html?index=..%2F..%2Findex#0>.

"Gradient Checking and Advanced Optimization." *Gradient Checking and
Advanced Optimization - Ufldl*. N.p., n.d. Web. 06 Jan. 2017.
<http://deeplearning.stanford.edu/wiki/index.php/Gradient_checking_and_advanced_optimization>.

"A Hackable Text Editor for the 21st Century." *Atom*. N.p., n.d. Web. 12
Dec. 2016. <https://atom.io/>.

Hamrick, Jessica. "An Introduction to Classes and Inheritance (in
Python)." *An Introduction to Classes and Inheritance (in Python) -
Jessica Hamrick*. N.p., 18 May 2011. Web. 11 Dec. 2016.

<http://www.jesshamrick.com/2011/05/18/an-introduction-to-classes-and-inheritance-in-python/>.

Heaton, Jeffery. *Introduction to the Math of Neural Networks*. N.p.: Heaton Research, 2012. 03 Apr. 2012. Web. 6 Dec. 2016. <https://www.amazon.com/Introduction-Math-Neural-Networks-Heaton-ebook/dp/B00845UQL6/ref=sr_1_1?ie=UTF8&qid=1481043122&sr=8-1&keywords=neural+network+math>.

Honchar, Oleksandr, and Luca Di Persio. "Artificial Neural Networks Approach to the Forecast of Stock Market Price Movements." N.p., Jan. 2016. Web. 15 Feb. 2017. <https://www.researchgate.net/publication/307639575_Artificial_neural_networks_approach_to_the_forecast_of_stock_market_price_movements>.

Hugolarochelle. "Neural Networks [1.1] : Feedforward Neural Network - Artificial Neuron." *YouTube*. YouTube, 16 Nov. 2013. Web. 17 Feb. 2017. <https://www.youtube.com/watch?v=SGZ6BttHMPw&index=1&list=PL6Xpj9I5qXYEcOhn7TqghAJ6NAPrNmUBH>.

Jiaconda. "A Concise History of Neural Networks." *Medium*. N.p., 29 Aug. 2016. Web. 14 Dec. 2016. <https://medium.com/@Jaconda/a-concise-history-of-neural-networks-2070655d3fec#.re2crs5mt>.

Khalid, Muhammad Yasoob Ullah. "20 Python Libraries You Can't Live without." *Python Tips*. N.p., 07 Aug. 2013. Web. 08 Dec. 2016. <https://pythontips.com/2013/07/30/20-python-libraries-you-cant-live-without/>.

Kohavi, Ron, and Foster Provost. "Glossary of Terms." *Glossary of Terms Journal of Machine Learning*. N.p., 1998. Web. 13 Dec. 2016. <http://robotics.stanford.edu/~ronnyk/glossary.html>.

"Library." *What Is Library? Webopedia Definition*. N.p., n.d. Web. 08 Dec. 2016. <http://www.webopedia.com/TERM/L/library.html>.

"Machine Learning." *Wikipedia*. Wikimedia Foundation, n.d. Web. 08 Dec. 2016. <https://en.wikipedia.org/wiki/Machine_learning>.

Marr, Bernard. "A Short History of Machine Learning -- Every Manager Should Read." *Forbes*. Forbes Magazine, 19 Feb. 2016. Web. 08 Dec. 2016. <http://www.forbes.com/sites/bernardmarr/2016/02/19/a-short-history-of-machine-learning-every-manager-should-read/#480b2f8f323f>.

Matthes, Eric. "Python Crash Course." *Python Crash Course by Ehmatthes*. N.p., n.d. Web. 08 Dec. 2016. <https://ehmatthes.github.io/pcc/cheatsheets/README.html>.

Mazur, Matt. "A Step by Step Backpropagation Example." *Matt Mazur*. N.p., 29 Apr. 2016. Web. 20 Dec. 2016. <https://mattmazur.com/2015/03/17/a-step-by-step-backpropagation-example/>.

MIT. "12a: Neural Nets." *YouTube*. YouTube, 20 Apr. 2016. Web. 23 Dec. 2016. <https://www.youtube.com/watch?v=uXt8qF2Zzfo&t=2097s>.

NyKamp, Duane. "Math Insight." *Parameter Definition - Math Insight*. N.p., n.d. Web. 28 Dec. 2016. <http://mathinsight.org/definition/parameter>.

"Python Data Analysis Library¶." *Python Data Analysis Library — Pandas: Python Data Analysis Library*. N.p., n.d. Web. 12 Dec. 2016. <http://pandas.pydata.org/>.

"Python Glossary." *Codecademy*. Codeacadmey, n.d. Web. 08 Dec. 2016. <https://www.codecademy.com/articles/glossary-python>.

Python Programming. Prod. Derek Banas. *YouTube*. N.p., 10 Nov. 2014. Web. 8 Dec. 2016. <https://www.youtube.com/watch?v=N4mEzFDjqtA>.

Rashid, Tariq. *Make Your Own Neural Network*. N.p.: n.p., 2016. 16 Apr. 2016. Web. 6 Dec. 2016. <https://www.amazon.com/Make-Your-Own-Neural-Network-ebook/dp/B01EER4Z4G/ref=pd_sim_351_6?_encoding=UTF8&psc=1&refRID=H3E0YQ1S1E3KMH048PQM>.

Rueckstiess, Thomas. "Welcome to PyBrain." *PyBrain*. N.p., n.d. Web. 12 Dec. 2016. <http://pybrain.org/>.

Ruder, Sebastian. "An Overview of Gradient Descent Optimization Algorithms." *Sebastian Ruder*. N.p., 17 Dec. 2016. Web. 23 Dec. 2016. <http://sebastianruder.com/optimizing-gradient-descent/index.html#gradientdescentvariants>.

Schapire, Rob. "What Is Machine Learning?" *Machine Learning* (2015): 01-16. Princeton University, 4 Feb. 2008. Web. 9 Dec. 2016. <http://www.cs.princeton.edu/courses/archive/spr08/cos511/scribe_notes/0204.pdf>.

"Scikit-learn." *Scikit-learn: Machine Learning in Python — Scikit-learn 0.18.1 Documentation*. N.p., n.d. Web. 12 Dec. 2016. <http://scikit-

learn.org/stable/>.

Sentdex. "Sentdex." *YouTube*. YouTube, n.d. Web. 03 Mar. 2017.
<https://www.youtube.com/channel/UCfzlCWGWYyIQ0aLC5w48g
BQ>.

"Siraj Raval." *YouTube*. YouTube, n.d. Web. 03 Mar. 2017.
<https://www.youtube.com/channel/UCWN3xxRkmTPmbKwht9Fu
E5A>.

"Stack Overflow." *Stack Overflow*. N.p., n.d. Web. 03 Mar. 2017.
<http://stackoverflow.com/>

"TensorFlow Is an Open Source Software Library for Machine
Intelligence." *TensorFlow - an Open Source Software Library for
Machine Intelligence*. N.p., n.d. Web. 12 Dec. 2016.
<https://www.tensorflow.org/>.

"Terminology Used in the Field of Neural Networks." Wiley, n.d. Web. 8
Dec. 2016.
<http://onlinelibrary.wiley.com/store/10.1002/9780470742624.app9/
asset/app9.pdf;jsessionid=34C0345A3FB0A3388EA69CA778C970
3C.f03t04?v=1&t=iwgt2bcl&s=9c127497976d14770e073e156d506
4e997bcd4f8>.

"Torch | Scientific Computing for LuaJIT." *Torch*. N.p., n.d. Web. 12 Dec.
2016. <http://torch.ch/>.

"Unsupervised Feature Learning and Deep Learning Tutorial."
Unsupervised Feature Learning and Deep Learning Tutorial.
Stanford University, n.d. Web. 09 Dec. 2016.
<http://ufldl.stanford.edu/tutorial/supervised/ConvolutionalNeuralN
etwork/>.

"Welcome¶." *Welcome — Theano 0.8.2 Documentation*. N.p., n.d. Web.
12 Dec. 2016. <http://deeplearning.net/software/theano/>.

"What Does "library" Mean in the Case of Programming Languages?"
N.p., n.d. Web. 8 Dec. 2016. <https://www.quora.com/What-does-
library-mean-in-the-case-of-programming-languages.

"Whats the Difference between a Module and a Library in Python?" *Stack
Overflow*. N.p., n.d. Web. 08 Dec. 2016.
<http://stackoverflow.com/questions/19198166/whats-the-
difference-between-a-module-and-a-library-in-python>.

Made in the USA
Lexington, KY
20 August 2019